"In the *Decoding Sylvia Plath* books, Gordon-Bramer deals the reader a full house out of the tarot deck, the occult, the Qabalah, mythology, and alchemy that leads both casual readers and critics alike to wonder just what they have overlooked amidst the general cacophony surrounding the circumstances of Plath's personal life and relationships. As the Grecian Fates once embroidered people's lives from the threads of fate, Gordon-Bramer weaves her mysticism into a cogent tapestry of deeper, transcendent interpretation of Plath's work and meaning in modern letters.
-Prof. Robert Masterson, CUNY-BMCC, New York City

"This is a friendly, conversational approach so that students won't feel overwhelmed, and it talks about topics that other guides don't, allowing students to make original, insightful commentary on the work. The study guide is a worthwhile, useful investment for students."
-Cathleen Allyn Conway, editor, *Plath Profiles: An Interdisciplinary Journal for Plath Studies*

Praise for *Fixed Stars Govern a Life: Decoding Sylvia Plath:*

"Julia Gordon-Bramer has written a staggering reinterpretation of Sylvia Plath…There has been a vacuum in Plath studies regarding her involvement with tarot, Qabalah, astrology and astronomy. Gordon-Bramer expertly argues her case."
-Rehan Qayoom, poet, editor, translator and archivist

"With clarity and erudition, Ms. Gordon-Bramer illuminates how Plath's masterpiece *Ariel* reflects a clear and intentional alignment with the Tarot and the Qabalah's Tree of Life. With each poem and the collection as a whole, Gordon-Bramer weaves the esoteric mysteries with historical interpretation in a fascinating scholarly analysis that is original, provocative, magical. *Fixed Stars Govern a Life* is an incantation of great resonance and power, and its publication will be a sensation."
-Susan L. Woods, Ph.D., Emeritus Professor of Women's Studies, Eastern Illinois University

"Like her beloved Yeats, Sylvia Plath was drawn to numerous and often contradictory systems of belief and ways of knowing, including mystical and magical systems. Julia Gordon-Bramer, in her dazzling and meticulously researched book, shows us how Sylvia Plath may have drawn upon the images of the tarot to fuse and merge the many ways of knowing she was so profoundly inspired by myth, science, current events, folklore, alchemy, literature, motherhood, art and other sources to create the poems in *Ariel*, one of the great literary achievement of the 20th century. In doing so, Julia Gordon-Bramer illuminates, expands on, and asks profound questions about the very nature of making and creating poems."
-Catherine Bowman, multiple prizewinner for poetry, and author of *The Plath Cabinet* and other collections

"A wonderful exploration of Plath's *Ariel* poems in relation to myth, symbol, and the creative process."
-Kathleen Connors, author of *Eye Rhymes: Sylvia Plath's Art of the Visual*

"Lucid and intriguing…what is valuable about *Fixed Stars Govern a Life* is that it is such a great source study with commentary on what Plath read, what was happening at the time of the poem, and more."
-Carl Rollyson, author of *American Isis: The Life and Art of Sylvia Plath*

"An intriguing book that prompts the reader to look at Plath with fresh eyes. *Fixed Stars Govern a Life* aims to explore the poet's hidden side and as such, it is a refreshingly welcome addition to Plath studies."
-Andrew Wilson, author of *Mad Girl's Love Song*

Praise for *Decoding Sylvia Plath's "Daddy"*:

"I am fascinated and intrigued by Julia Gordon-Bramer's wildly and dizzyingly original readings of Sylvia Plath's poems. Not only does she make me realize that I need to go back and read the poems again, she comes pretty close to convincing me that I have really never read them at all."
-Troy Jollimore, National Book Critics Circle Award for Poetry, Guggenheim Fellowship for Creative Arts Recipient

"Julia Gordon-Bramer's *Decoding Sylvia Plath's 'Daddy'* presents the iconic poet in full three-dimensional view. Or six-dimensional, if you prefer. This Sylvia Plath is far more than the depressive, suicidal drama queen and father-hater depicted in easier accounts of the poet's life. Plath emerges as the genius's genius. Ms. Bramer's tone adds enjoyment to her already rigorous and penetrating work."
-Robert Nazarene, founding editor, *The American Journal of Poetry*

Decoding Sylvia Plath's "Lady Lazarus"

FREEDOM'S FEMININE FIRE

INCLUDES A GUIDE FOR STUDENTS AND TEACHERS

Julia Gordon-Bramer

St. Louis, Missouri

Copyright ©2017 by Julia Gordon-Bramer

All rights reserved. No part of this publication may be reproduced, distributed or transmitted in any form or by any means, including photocopying, recording, or other electronic or mechanical methods, without the prior written permission of the publisher, except in the case of brief quotations embodied in critical reviews and certain other noncommercial uses permitted by copyright law. For permission requests, write to the publisher, addressed "Attention: Permissions Coordinator," at the address below:

Magi Press
331 N. New Ballas Road #410176
St. Louis, Missouri 63141-9998 USA
(314) 529-3904

Ordering Information:

Quantity sales. Special discounts are available on quantity purchases by corporations, associations, and others. For details, contact the "Special Sales Department" at the address above.

Editing by BookEval.com
Cover design from a WWI U.S. Liberty Bonds poster in the Public Domain.

Publisher's Cataloging-In-Publication Data
(Prepared by The Donohue Group, Inc.)

Names: Gordon-Bramer, Julia.
Title: Decoding Sylvia Plath's "Lady Lazarus" : freedom's feminine fire / Julia Gordon-Bramer.
Description: St. Louis, Missouri : Magi Press, [2017] | Series: Decoding Sylvia Plath's-- | "Includes a Guide for Students and Teachers." | Includes bibliographical references.
Identifiers: ISBN 9780999186039 | ISBN 9780999186015 (ebook)
Subjects: LCSH: Plath, Sylvia. Poems--Criticism, Textual. | Feminism in literature. | Liberty in literature. | Mysticism in literature.
Classification: LCC PS3566.L27 D344 2017 (print) | LCC PS3566.L27 (ebook) | DDC 811/.54--dc23

Acknowledgements

Thanks to Tom, who continues to amaze me with his support and hard work. The task of publishing more than forty Plath books ahead(!) feels overwhelming, and I could not do it without you. Thanks to Zulf for always pushing me. You are the best reading and writing mentor ever. Thanks to Tom Reynolds for continued friendship, belief in this work and me, and signature-wrangling in the eleventh hour.

I continue to be grateful to my graduate students in the creative writing program at Lindenwood who tested each and every lesson plan out and helped expand upon the work. With Lindenwood in mind, thanks and blessings to Dr. Michael Castro, professor emeritus and the first poet laureate of St. Louis, who I've known since my days hosting Ken Kesey, Gloria Steinem and the incomparable Allen Ginsberg for the Writer's Voice of the West County YMCA. Dr. Castro led me to serve on the board of the wonderful *River Styx* literary magazine where I served for several years, and he brought me in to present on "Lady Lazarus" even before *Fixed Stars Govern a Life: Decoding Sylvia Plath* was out. He *got it* right off the bat. For this book especially, extra thanks goes to my former students Troy Casa, David Gilmore and Theresa (Ti) Sumner, who expanded on the sections of Exploring the Connections, Mythology, Alchemy and History. And Ti, in addition to your genius comments, your early readings and friendship have been a treasure to me. Students can be the best teachers! I continue to learn from my friend, the excellent poet and teacher Catherine Bowman, who has brought me in to her classrooms at Indiana University-Bloomington to speak on Plath, "Lady Lazarus" in particular, and the tarot many times. Thanks also to Davida Federman for her knowledge of Mesoamerican studies.

A shout out of gratitude to BookEval.com, who challenged me to prove every finding. Sometimes, with mysticism, we get the answers before we can explain in layman's terms exactly how we got there.

I'd like to also use this space for my appreciation of the great resources and tools available to prove that path: As always, a great debt for the hours sitting in the Sylvia Plath archives at the Lilly Library, Indiana University-Bloomington. For this and all of my Plath books, past and future, I owe a great debt to the great body of work by Karen V. Kukil and Peter K. Steinberg for some of my resources: *The Unabridged Journals of Sylvia Plath*, *The Letters of Sylvia Plath, Volume One: 1940-1956*, the Sylvia Plath Information Blog, the website "A Celebration This Is!" and The Sylvia Plath collection on LibraryThing. The newly-released *Letters*, especially, has been such a gift to this work. All of Sylvia Plath's connections and sources can be found in these places, it just took a while (ten years!) to find and read everything. These aforementioned resources have saved me many hours and dollars in archival visits. Also, what would we do without the Internet, Google, and Wikipedia? While it's always smart to double-check, they're invaluable tools. Those of you practicing qabalistic connections in your own artistic work can take advantage of Wikipedia's disambiguation pages as a source. Plath would have loved this, although it seems her mind just did it naturally. Thanks also to the used book and magazine sellers who helped build my library of what Plath read. And donate! That's good energy.

On a personal level, I can ditto everyone else in the acknowledgments from the *Decoding Sylvia Plath's "Daddy" book*, published at the same time as this one. Love, love, love!

Contents

What You Should Know Going In 3
About the Poem "Lady Lazarus" 9
First Mirror: Tarot and Qabalah 21
Second Mirror: Alchemy 37
Third Mirror: Mythology 49
Fourth Mirror: History and World Events 61
Fifth Mirror: Astrology and Astronomy 77
Sixth Mirror: The Arts and Humanities 85
Decoding Sylvia Plath's "Lady Lazarus" in the Classroom 105
Bibliography 119

For
the strong women
who came before me

Decoding Sylvia Plath's "Lady Lazarus"

"There are a whole lot of things in this world of ours you haven't started wondering about yet."

—Roald Dahl, *James and the Giant Peach*

CHAPTER ONE

What You Should Know Going In

"Your daughter shall start her way on the road to becoming a seeress and will also learn how to do horoscopes, a very difficult art, which means reviving my elementary math…"
—Sylvia Plath, in a letter to her mother, October 23, 1956

Suppose that someone, or a group of someones, decided that the entirety of who you are is based almost exclusively on some things you wrote and a couple of events. Limiting, right? Even if some of the information is true, people are complicated. We have moods and roles that we play in certain situations. We have how we see ourselves, and how we would like to see ourselves, which isn't always how others perceive us. Sylvia Plath wanted to be perfect in all things, and we know that in her later years, as she grew more confident in her success as a writer, it seems that she wrote her letters and journals often with the foreknowledge that they would one day be read. What one person wants to express, especially in writing, is a controlled thing, like an online personality or a public-relations image. If you're old enough to read this, you're probably wise enough to know that our politicians, celebrities, and even our friends all present carefully crafted images for the public. Maybe you do, too, keeping some things private.

We can all admit that we sometimes knowingly or unknowingly use the power of suggestion on others, and we are continually influenced by powerful words in advertising, politics, and so on. Psychologists and hypnotherapists are well aware of the power of suggestion. In one experiment, researchers asked groups to watch a film of a car driving through the countryside. The viewers were then asked questions: "Did the car speed past the white barn? Was the blonde at the wheel driving recklessly?" The viewers responded with vivid memories about the barn and the blonde, although no buildings or blonde existed in the movie at all. Suggestion changes our perception, and it can limit what you notice and also create false memories. I am going to show you that you have been indoctrinated in this same way. That school told you what to believe and think about Sylvia Plath, and because of this, you've missed the point of her work altogether. I am going to amaze you with the plain truth that has been right in front of your eyes all along.

If you're a new reader of Plath, you've probably heard the basic bio: Sylvia Plath is a world-famous American-born poet who made her name in the late 1950s and early '60s (but became most famous posthumously). She might, unfortunately, be best-known for her drama: her tough marriage to poet Ted Hughes, and her infamous suicide. Because of this story, much of the world has interpreted Plath's work through a limited, autobiographical view, interpreting her poems literally based on her journals, letters, and her novel, *The Bell Jar*. Plath is described as "confessional," "angry," "depressive," and sometimes also as having written "feminist" literature. End of story. And that miserable story hasn't changed in fifty years.

Let's get ready to change the story.

Sylvia Plath's poetry is powerful, and yet few understand *why*. Her fans seem to increase with the years and across the globe, along with her notoriety. Movies about her, or based on her work, continue to be made. Plath was beautiful, adding to her star quality, and her photographs are widely traded and adorn countless web pages. Gossipy newspaper and magazine articles are published to this day about problems in her marriage, her sexual exploits and proclivities, lost poems, found carbon papers: you name it. We can't seem to get enough of her. It is not that Plath didn't have drama, or even that some of those autobiographical elements aren't also within her work. But if you're reading Plath seeing only that, you're missing out on most of it.

Psychologists say that all of us are guilty of summing up people: having the mistaken belief that the traits or actions that we see tell the entire story. It is a tendency called the "Fundamental Attribution Error." People overestimate the importance of looks and behaviors and underestimate the importance of the situation and context. We look for a "dispositional" explanation instead of a contextual one. There is something about us that makes us want to explain our world in terms of character and the labels we give them (kind, smart, loving, angry, and so on), discounting the critically important environmental cues and circumstances.

So how do you know that I'm not doing the same thing here, attempting to imprint my particular view upon Plath's persona? Right now, you don't. But I'm going to prove it to you, step by step.

This book is going to shine a light on the layers of Plath's famous poem "Lady Lazarus," peeling off its layers as Plath's napkin image is peeled away in her fourth stanza, so you can understand the poem in all its glory. You will soon see that this poem is not just a love letter to suicide. In fact, it's really not about that at all. Plath had the gift of layering meanings, *meanings of context*, in her work that tell the stories around her: stories of her history, events of her time, mythology, and so much more. So much meaning hides beneath that too-easy literal life-story interpretation, which never really did work out the nitty-gritty details unless you factor in poetic license or just call Plath an occasional liar. It is time to reveal her deeper themes and context.

When you finish this book, you'll be able to understand that "Lady Lazarus" is about femininity—full-blast! It's a poem about the first women (there were two) and the fall of man in the Garden of Eden. This poem is also about the real-life Liliths: Lady Shark Fin, Emma Lazarus, and Sojourner Truth. It's about the goddess and the planet Venus, and her many, many names, which include Lucifer and Isis. It's a poem about women's struggles, not only across the ages but across the races, and how females are all "the same, identical woman." "Lady Lazarus" is a poem about freedom and equality and its symbolic representation, which most especially features the Statue of Liberty.

How can one poem be about so many different things at once? I'll show you how Plath's words do sextuple-duty, how Plath was a genius's genius. You're going to understand soon the context around Plath and her work, which changes everything you previously believed to be true.

The full text of Plath's poem "Lady Lazarus" can be found in *Ariel: The Restored Edition* (2004, Harper Perennial Modern Classics), pages 14-17, or, I am sure, with a web search. "Lady Lazarus" is certainly one of Plath's best-known and most-studied poems, and there is a terrific recording Plath made of it, easily found online. If you know anything about "Lady Lazarus," this is what we might call one of her greatest hits; in fact, it's widely considered to be one of the greatest contemporary American poems. English professors and students of literature have probably read Plath's "Lady Lazarus" fifty or a hundred times as a model of the confessional poem. Many of us know it by heart. And why not? It seems to be the ultimate summary of a life: family history, vengeance, and resurrection. We get *that* much.

> "The modern woman: demands as much experience as the modern man."
> –Sylvia Plath

A few brief notes:

Most of the information in this book draws from the *Fixed Stars Govern a Life: Decoding Sylvia Plath* system, by myself, Julia Gordon-Bramer, although the work on this poem has been expanded and revised as I and my Lindenwood University graduate students continued to make discoveries. *Fixed Stars Govern a Life: Decoding Sylvia Plath,* Volume One (referred to from here on as *FSGL*) was published in 2014 by Stephen F. Austin State University Press. Over the next few years, I will reissue an expanded and revised book about each poem first decoded in Volume One, as well as release the never-before-seen *FSGL* interpretations for the poems that would be part of Volume Two.

Decodings of Plath's *Ariel* poems are scheduled for publication with Magi Press in small individual books like this one, part of the *Decoding* series available in ebook and paperback format (and eventually audiobook, too). These small books allow me to have a bit more freedom and fun with the poems, dropping the academic tone, while also providing the space to take them apart and peel off each layer of meaning. All in all, it makes for easier reading. *Decoding Sylvia Plath's "Lady Lazarus"* is a book for everyone because Plath is for everyone.

Sylvia Plath and her husband Ted Hughes had an intense interest in mysticism and the occult, from casting horoscopes from the stars to conjuring spirits through the Ouija board. Plath had her own tarot deck, was photographed holding a crystal ball, and a plethora of her published and unpublished journal notes and letters support these passions. Expect to be astounded when you see all that the mystical *context* reveals. To view Plath's work this way is to turn a light on in a dark place, and you might be pleasantly surprised to learn that Plath is not merely the dreary poet you thought she was. You're going to see that Plath's *Ariel* collection corresponds in perfect order to the tarot, which aligns with the Qabalah's Tree of Life. Right now, I realize that's a lot of words you probably don't understand. That's okay. You will.

When you finish with this book, you will know that Plath's work is a lot more than just depressive reflections, confessional autobiography, and wishes for suicide. As you pull apart "Lady Lazarus" with me, you will find easily verifiable facts that are a little too coincidental to be called chance. You will understand Plath's choice of words, and how images that she has been criticized for, such as her Jewish and Holocaust references, were exactly right for her purpose.

Warning: If you picked this book up wanting only a quick summary of what is already known and has been said about "Lady Lazarus" a million times, stop reading here. *Decoding Sylvia Plath's "Lady Lazarus"* is not a book for the uninterested student looking for a quick answer for a passing grade. But for those of you who get excited about the power of the written word, buckle up! You're about to see every traditional interpretation challenged. This book provides a mystical and contextual perspective that reveals everything. You will soon see just how close-minded academia has been, and that Plath has been essentially read wrongly for more than fifty years. This is a book to kick a Plath fan's ass (in the best possible way), and it builds a heck of a case for mysticism too.

If you never knew much about Sylvia Plath before now, you will soon understand this poem, "Lady Lazarus," better than most scholars today. After a few *Decoding* books, you might begin to see mystical patterns in other artists' works too. I hope you'll review this book online, tell your friends, and blog about it. By the end of this book, I promise you that you'll never see this poem, or Sylvia Plath, in the same light again.

For more details on my decoding process, please read the introduction to *FSGL*, which can be found at no cost to you at https://lindenwood.academia.edu/JuliaGordonBramer.

Please note: Because of copyright restrictions, the poem "Lady Lazarus" is not reprinted here. Partial quotes and references are made as permitted.

CHAPTER TWO

About the Poem "Lady Lazarus"

It's about wanting to commit suicide, right?

Actually, no. "Lady Lazarus" is the poem that first comes to everyone's minds when discussing Sylvia Plath's suicidal tendency. What most people do not understand is that it is the primary goal of mysticism (and even some religions, such as Buddhism) to kill the weak, impure human ego in order to rise again as a superior being of the spirit. This ego death and resurrection is the journey of Initiation.

"Abandon my ego," Plath wrote in her journal numerous times. You might or might not be interested in matters of the occult with regard to your own life. But the facts are that Plath and her husband Ted Hughes surely were. This journey of Initiation is illustrated in the tarot, beginning with The Fool card and ending twenty-one cards later with The World. But first, let's bring it back down to the real world and get some context:

It was October 1962, the month that Plath wrote "Lady Lazarus." A week before she began the infamous *Ariel* October poems (which are arguably the strongest in that collection), she received a copy of her close friend Anne Sexton's collection of poetry, *All My Pretty Ones*. Sexton is also ranked as one of the major confessional poets, right up there with Plath. In *All My Pretty Ones*, Sexton plays with some of the same rhythms, dark tones, and dangerous suicidal musings. In this collection, Sexton equates women with Lucifer in her poem "Ghosts," and even uses Lazarus imagery in her poem "The Hangman":

> Those six times that you almost died
> the newest medicine and the family fuss
> pulled you back again. Supplied
> with air, against my guilty wish,
> your clogged pipes cried
> like Lazarus.

The seeds had been planted. Sexton obviously inspired Plath's images and tone for "Lady Lazarus." As in Plath's poem, we see here repeated attempts at suicide, the idea of being brought back, and of course, the name "Lazarus." But it doesn't stop there. Not by a long shot.

As you may already know, Sylvia Plath grew up in the United States during World War II. Movies in the theater were a primary form of entertainment, and, before television, theaters showed newsreels about the news of the day, including the war. Plath learned that her family heritage represented the enemy. Plath's mother Aurelia was Austrian, and her father Otto was German-Prussian. Her heritage outwardly explains why "Lady Lazarus" is weighted with negative examples of German culture. We see the Nazi party and hints of their terrible crimes against humanity (Nazi lampshades made of skin, paperweights made of bone, linen fabric woven from hair). There is the sexist, paternalistic weight of the German language itself, seen in the words "Herr" and "Doktor," which we will discuss later. It is a language that Plath struggled to learn into her young adult years. You will see that the German language surfaces again in her later *Ariel* poem, "Daddy."

When Plath was in high school, her class took a trip to Germany, in part to see the famous Passion Play in Oberammergau, Germany. Plath's family could not afford to send her on this expensive journey, and we can speculate that this was hard on her because she was such a social person involved in all school events.

Of course, you already get the sense that "Lady Lazarus" is a feminist poem. How could it not be, with that last line "And I eat men like air"? Hughes wrote, "Sylvia's poems & novel hit the first militant wave of Feminism as a divine revelation from their Patron Saint." What you, and they, might not have understood was that Plath was steeped in feminism from the cradle. Her mother Aurelia was once a suffragette, marching for the right to vote. Plath went to Smith College, a prestigious women's college in Northampton, Massachusetts, where she was not only encouraged but expected to succeed. Smith produced many role models for Plath in their long list of notable alumnae, including Otelia Cromwell, Margaret Mitchell, Anne Morrow Lindbergh, Julia Child, Madeleine L'Engle, and Betty Friedan. Amelia Earhart's sister Muriel was also "a Smith girl," and the famous aviator visited her sister on campus often.

The facts are that no one ever told young Sylvia Plath that there was anything she could not accomplish, and so she pretty much achieved everything she set her mind to, winning prizes and scholarships, publications and awards, and every enviable position in clubs, on the school newspaper, and in student government.

In the fall of 1959, Plath and her husband Ted Hughes stayed a few months at the Yaddo arts colony in New York State. They had returned to the U.S. from England the previous year by ship, passing the Statue of Liberty in the harbor at New York City. Ah, but Plath had noticed and written of this statue well before Hughes came into her life, in 1954:

> "after this, all I could take was a long windy ride on the Staten Island ferry, [...] watching the glittering skyline of Manhattan recede and the statue of liberty grow green and big, and then the statue dwindle, and the lights rise tall and shining above us in the windy dark…"

It was most likely at Yaddo that Plath wrote her poem "The Colossus," the title poem in her first published collection of poetry. Plath's "The Colossus" addresses the Colossus of Rhodes, a gigantic statue portraying a male god, which was one of the seven wonders of the ancient world. Plath's "The Colossus" is widely interpreted to be a metaphor for the destruction of and piecing together of memories around her father, using this statue as a metaphor.

So what does her older poem "The Colossus" have to do with "Lady Lazarus"? I'm getting to that: At the base of the Statue of Liberty is a poem entitled "The New Colossus," written by Jewish poet Emma Lazarus (you read that last name right). Plath saw this statue of a grand feminine goddess as a transformative icon for the power of women, rooted in the goddess Isis and all of her incarnations around the world. "Lady Lazarus," therefore, became Plath's *second* Colossus poem. "Lady Lazarus" is a tribute to the new Colossus, to women, and to her new self. All overcame great adversity.

Meanwhile, when Plath wrote "Lady Lazarus" in October 1962, the Cold War with the Soviet Union was in full swing, and Germany had been divided by the Berlin Wall. Once again, family motherland (or part of it, anyway) was the enemy.

Invited to read her poems on British radio (BBC) in December 1962, Plath presented her poems almost as stories with characters. She was rather vague, and put distance between her poems and her personal life. In her notes prefacing the poems, found on pages 195-197 of *Ariel: The Restored Edition*, Plath gave the BBC the following introduction to "Lady Lazarus," which may have been closer to the truth than some of her other introductions:

> "…The speaker is a woman who has the great and terrible gift of being reborn. the only trouble is, she has to die first. She is the

phoenix, the libertarian spirit, what you will. She is also just a good, plain, resourceful woman."

It is that last line, about the "good, plain, resourceful woman" that I want you to hold in your mind as you read along. You're going to understand how important these words are.

Imagine if I painted a baseball half black. If I hold up the black side toward you and ask you what color it is, you will say "black." If I hold up the white side, you will say "white." If I hold up the side where it is divided, you will say "black and white." This little analogy explains why it is important to view the same thing or idea from different vantage points before you take a stance. The bigger lesson, of course, is never to let someone tell you how to think. Not your schools, not your media, and not even me. I am going to show you six sides to "Lady Lazarus" that no one has ever seen before. You are going to see how they all work together to tell us a greater story. Ultimately, you are going to draw your own conclusions. I think you will agree with Plath that this poem is a story about the "good, plain, resourceful woman."

We are fascinated by and study Plath's work because it gets and holds our attention. This book, and the rest of the *Decoding* series, attempts to show you the six dimensions of Plath's poetry which speak to the spirit and the subconscious. You will soon learn not only what's there, but *how* it affects you. If you've read this far, you already know this poem is not an ode to death. Are you ready to peel off the veil of "Lady Lazarus," and reveal the spell which Plath has put upon us all?

Unless you're a regular with tarot and Qabalah, I might use a word or two that sounds unfamiliar and intimidating. Relax. As we travel through, I'll explain the points you need to know as simply as possible. Soon, the structure and meanings of Plath's work will make perfect sense to you, and you will wonder how no one had seen this before.

The Structure of a Spell

If you've read Plath's *Ariel: The Restored Edition*, you have already experienced a sense of flow between one poem and the next. Would you like to know how she did it?

In my first book, *Fixed Stars Govern a Life: Decoding Sylvia Plath, Volume One* (2014, Stephen F. Austin State University Press), I explain how poetry is a kind of an incantation. In a 1956 letter to Sylvia Plath, her husband Ted Hughes coached Plath on how the brain learns from hearing. Not surprising, then, that Plath was adamant that her poems were: "written for the ear, not the eye: they are poems written out loud."

"Lady Lazarus" is a terrific example of this with its steady repetition of sound: *I, I, I, It's, It's, It's, A, A, A, So, so, so, Herr, Herr, Herr*...These sometimes harsh triple-poundings imitate psychotherapeutical techniques. Want an example? Think of that wonderful scene near the end of the movie *Good Will Hunting*, where Robin Williams says over and over to Matt Damon until Damon reaches his emotional breaking point, "It's not your fault. It's not your fault. It's not your fault."

Hypnosis in the written and spoken word has been a powerful tool for many poets and prophets. When Hughes was talking about Plath's *Ariel* to Keith Sagar in a letter, he explained:

> "That's a hypnotic technique (which Crowley[1] used to like to demonstrate)—imitating somebody, exactly, until, at some imperceptible point, the initiative passes to you & they begin to imitate you, & can then be controlled—it's the fundamental dynamics of the artistic process, but in literature nowhere so naked as in those Ariel poems, which are all little dramas. More like some painting, or music, than any other poetry."

I'll be using examples from psychology and even hypnosis to show you not only how Plath's work affects your emotions, but also how

---

[1] Aleister Crowley (1875-1929), English occultist, ceremonial magician, poet, painter, novelist and mountaineer. An early member of the Hermetic Order of the Golden Dawn, he founded the religion of Thelema and proclaimed himself a prophet.

the world has programmed you to think of Plath's work in extremely limited terms.

But back to incantations: In "Lady Lazarus," we know that there has been repetition from the first line, "I have done it again." We know this even before we know what "it" is. Soon after we learn of the cat's "nine times to die. This is number three." The poem that precedes "Lady Lazarus" is "Barren Woman," with the word *echo* in its first line. "Lady Lazarus," with its repetition, has a kind of an echo too. An echo of sorts opens both poems.

About Plath's *Ariel* poems, Hughes said:

> "It is based on a psychic map—an actual drawing, which is also a sort of calibrated register between the two extreme poles of her system—of her double personality. Each of her poems can be placed pretty well exactly on the register by simply reading off the evident psychic components—her very systematized and consistent hierogylphs, and fitting them to the calibration. At one extreme are the frigidly brittle self-protective. At the other extreme, the rawest of Ariel."

"Lady Lazarus" is one of the rawest of *Ariel*.

Evidently, in "Lady Lazarus" both death and resurrection have taken place twice before. Plath foreshadows a continued cycle in her first line.

The echoing images in "Barren Woman" represent something leaving and returning without change. That idea plays, in two ways, into the 12th-stanza "Lazy Lazarus" line: "Nevertheless, I am the same, identical woman." The first is the obvious, literal interpretation of dying and being resurrected as the same woman—a theme Plath often explores as she seeks transcendence as a higher, ego-less self. The second meaning is ascending from an earthly form to spiritual formlessness, and then descending back into the original form as a forever-changed being. Same person, but different. Like losing your virginity, or un-seeing the movie of Stephen King's *It*.[2]

---

[2] Author note: I haven't actually gone to see *It*. I'm too scared.

Plath told the BBC that her latest poems had been created for the voice rather than for the page: She explained about her writing process, "whatever lucidity they may have comes from the fact that I say them to myself." In the introduction for this and other poems in this performance (she read "Daddy," "Medusa," "Lady Lazarus," "Nick and the Candlestick," and "Ariel"), remember that Plath commented that they should be understood as emerging from that voice of an invented character, not as poems about herself. As titillating as it is to think otherwise, and boy, the world loves to be titillated with gossip about Plath!—you will soon see that there is a great deal of evidence to support that she told the truth that day.

Our brains work not by absorbing information in quantities like a sponge, but through connections and associations. We learn and understand based on previous facts and memories to which we can relate the new information. One connection builds from another, often unconsciously. That's why it might be hard to accept if I tell you that Plath's poems are incantations, because what do you know about the occult? Maybe nothing. Maybe a little. Maybe a lot. And so it is essential that I must prove it to you. As I said earlier, because it is foolish to take someone's word for it, I will show you, connection by connection, so that you can make up your own mind.

In the same way that I will show you the connections in "Lady Lazarus," each Plath poem in *Ariel* sets up the next one through key words and associations. With each line, our knowledge and awareness develops. We travel with Plath and evolve together as we read.

Was Plath's mind really so massive as to process six thematically united yet unique perspectives at once? It could be argued that she processed even more than six meanings at one time because she managed to relate each poem to a current circumstance in her life without letting the poem become *about* her life.

Discovering the Connections

Whether it was intentional or not, many words, images, and themes are loaded into Plath's *Ariel* poems, and these themes seep out of one poem and run into the next. This connectedness undoubtedly contributes to a subconscious unification of themes and flow of information to keep the reader spellbound beyond the power of the rhythms and symbolism. Remember when I said you'll see a lot of psychology in this and other books in the *Decoding* series? That's because psychology is how the mind works, and mysticism, illusion, even faith all depend on the mind and perception. "Perception is 9/10 of the law," says hypnotherapist Kevin Hogan. "What we believe we see to be true is what we consider to be true. We don't test our perceptions to see if they are true. We just perceive and assume stuff is real."

Psychologist Carl Jung coined the term *synchronicity* to describe what he called the *acausal connecting principle*. It is a meaningful connection between inner and outer events which defy explanation. It's unbelievable coincidence. It is a glimpse into the underlying order of the universe. In Qabalah and much of mysticism, everything is said to be connected.

It is no coincidence that in viewing the connecting words, images, and themes across Plath's first seven *Ariel* poems, we see a quest toward a famous public image that leaves only emptiness in the end. Or is this emptiness the beginning?

It's worth taking a look at "Lady Lazarus" as being "set up" by the previous *Ariel* poem, "Barren Woman." Both of these poems connect with the following ideas: blank faces, an audience and a public, feet and footfall, woman and womanhood, deadness and death, concern and attention, nothing and that nothing can happen. The leaping and returning fountain image in "Barren Woman" is a clear mirror of the ascending and descending form of the speaker in "Lady Lazarus."

Interesting, isn't it? And it continues: Plath's "Lady Lazarus" and the poem that follows it, "Tulips," share the connecting words of *red*, *heart, eye, cat, air, bright, pure, baby, face, skin,* and *black*. The connecting ideas are references to the age of thirty, unwrapping, surgeons, having no face, and managing one's own behavior. Skip around *Ariel*. You'll see that other poems in the collection might have one or two of these associations, but they are not linked or repeated to this extent.

You're going to see a lot about a "Triple Goddess" in the Mythology mirror of this book. Plath played with this idea also in her long poem, "Three Women." The Triple Goddess is the expression of the female in her three life stages of maiden, mother, and crone. As one version of her dies, she becomes the next. The female child dies to become the virginal young woman. The woman dies to become the mother. The mother dies to become the crone. She has a million different names, depending on the myth and in what part of the world that myth originated. Robert Graves's famous book, *The White Goddess*, is about the Triple Goddess. You'll know her mother side as Venus, Hera, or Gaia. You might have heard names for the maiden such as Aphrodite or Persephone. And the crone, which is such an impolite term: Let's instead call her "The mature woman." She is Isis, or Athene, or Lucifer.

The thing about this Triple Goddess, whatever her name, is that her phases of life run in order through Plath's *Ariel* collection too. "Thalidomide," the fourth *Ariel* poem, is that mother persona, grieving her child, as it were. In "The Applicant," we see the nubile maiden secretary, ripe to be picked for marriage. In "Barren Woman," she is old and empty, mother of a mother (Nike) and grandchildren. And what of "Lady Lazarus"? Well, she is our Triple Goddess, the opus or summation of them all.

Oh, and in case you didn't already know: *Ariel* was first published in 1965 in a reordered version edited by Ted Hughes after Plath's death. The loss of Plath's intended order meant that the hidden connections and synchronicity of the book's original design went unnoticed until after *Ariel: The Restored Edition, a Facsimile of*

Plath's Manuscript, Reinstating Her Original Selection and Arrangement, was published in 2004 by HarperPerennial.

There is some division as to whether events of intuition, precognition, or clairvoyance are the same as Jung's synchronicity, but we know from their writings and journals that Plath and Hughes both considered Plath to be highly psychic. Science has proven that at deep levels, everything is caught and united within a web of information that transcends time and space. Is synchronicity just a happy coincidence? Plath did it in her *Ariel* collection *forty times*, organized in a specific mystical order (the Tree of Life). A Harvard mathematician did the numbers for me and said for that to be chance is impossible. You can see the actual equation for this in the introduction to *Fixed Stars Govern a Life*. But even if you don't have the first book, this one will give you the knowledge and tools you need to see Plath's work, and this world, with new eyes to make up your own mind.

Before you get too hung up on the fact that you don't know tarot, or mythology, or alchemy, or whatever, to properly understand for yourself what I'm about to present, relax. I'm giving you the high-level overviews in plain language. Also, all of this stuff is easily verifiable through any Google search. Check it out yourself; don't just take my word for it.

CHAPTER THREE

First Mirror: Tarot and Qabalah

What are Tarot and Qabalah?

> "I must meantime this June beginning, learn about planets & horoscopes to be in the proper starred house: I'll wish I had learned if I don't: tarot pack, too. Maybe I should stay alone, unparalysed, & work myself into mystic & clairvoyant trances […] I can. Will."
> —Sylvia Plath

Don't let yourself be intimidated by the weirdness of the Q-word. It's difficult, I know. I'll break it down for you here first because you can't possibly understand why it matters and what the qabalistic references in Plath's work are if you don't first know what Qabalah is—in the most general sort of way. Think of Qabalah as a kind of language.

Language is what we have when we attach words or signs to thoughts and feelings, give things names, and find a way to communicate beyond pointing and emoting. Language distinguishes the vague term *plant* from the more specific *sunflower*. Language tells us more than that it is *daytime*, but precisely *high noon*. We have an idea and need language to express that idea. There are many languages widely used today and many long gone, and they all do or did this expression work. The Qabalah is a God-system. Think of it as the idea. Tarot is one of the many languages spoken by Qabalah. Tarot is a picture language with other occult languages built in, such as numerology, alchemy, mythology, and astrology. Even the actual human language of Hebrew is a part of tarot. The relationship between tarot and Hebrew is because Qabalah began as *Kabbalah*, ancient Jewish mysticism.

Tarot works like the flash cards you used in elementary school. For example, they prompted you to read the word *apple* next to a picture of that fruit. You had the capacity of judgment, even as a child, to know that the flash card was not an actual apple, but that the flashcard named and pictured an apple. In this same way, tarot is not Qabalah, but the cards reflect the Qabalah system. Plath used six clear languages or reflections of the Qabalah, which I call *Mirrors* in the *FSGL Decoding* system. This chapter that you're reading now addresses the first mirror: Tarot and Qabalah. The rest of the mirrors are Alchemy, Mythology, History and the World, Astrology and Astronomy, and the Arts and Humanities. Each Plath poem in *Ariel* astoundingly addresses all six of these mirrors. The mirrors unite with each other through the theme of its corresponding tarot card.

This is why Qabalah matters. It teaches us to see that Plath's poems all have six different yet related meanings. The tarot is our decoding book for the *Ariel* poems. Are you with me so far?

In 2007, when I first began decoding Plath's work, I knew nothing except that I had identified a lot of tarot imagery within the *Ariel* poems. I have been reading tarot cards since I was sixteen, so of course, I would be the one to see it. I thought my work would stop there. I did not expect this idea to change the course of my entire life. For a school project, I first began to identify the tarot card to which each *Ariel* poem corresponded. That task proved to be fairly easy, as Plath placed her poems all in tarot order, the order she first intended for her book. I found materials in archives, and in other published materials, to support Plath's occult endeavors. The first published version of *Ariel* was rearranged by Plath's husband, Ted Hughes. He published Plath's collection posthumously, and so the tarot/Qabalah synchronicities went unnoticed for almost fifty years. We see Plath's intended order in *Ariel: The Restored Edition*.

I thought that was it: that Plath most creatively disguised a collection of tarot poems. After all, she had a tarot deck of her own, which she even mentions in the poem "Daddy." This discovery would have been a big deal by itself because no one was talking about it. What more could there be?

Plath's ordering and imagery were impressive, no doubt. But then something else commanded my attention: as I applied the meaning of each card to each poem, I noticed a lot of chemical and elemental names, like Air, the Sea, Mercury, Tin, and Gold. And colors like red, white and black. Over and over. So much repetition. Weird, right?

The chemicals and elements led me to the subject of alchemy. Believe me. I didn't want to go there. I have never taken a chemistry course in my life. Next thing I knew, I began to identify planetary references, which brought me of course to astrology and astronomy. I saw the same stories from mythology show up in Plath's current events and then echoed again in the arts that she appreciated. When would the correspondences end? Maybe they don't. How deep do Plath's poems go?

Little did I know I had fallen headlong into the world of Qabalah. While Plath didn't have any Qabalah books in her personal library, she had tons on Mormonism. Voila! Joseph Smith, founder of the Mormon Church and his connection to the occult, and Kabbalah (they spell it with a K) especially, has been widely written about. This is background that even the average Mormon doesn't know unless they've done historical research (which Plath *had* done). It is much like most modern Jews don't know they have roots in this same mysticism. Beyond the books on the Mormon Church, there are many more in the Plath archives addressing Qabalah, alchemy and Rosicrucianism, and many other forms of mysticism. Over the years of reading these same books Plath owned and read, I began to understand just how dizzyingly magical Plath's poems are. All statements are backed up with the sources from Plath's own library, found in this book's bibliography. I will teach it to you here. The most important thing is that just knowing the corresponding tarot card's meaning unlocks Plath's poem. For "Lady Lazarus," that is The Lovers card.

Next, keep in mind that the words and ideas Plath uses over and over in her poetry reflect greater patterns seen across the world in history, in mythology, in our environment, in the stars, and even in the arts and science. She explains this layering of themes in her own letters. In 1954 she wrote this about an earlier poem, "Dirge in Three Parts":

> "Of course the first verse is supposed to derive from a small satire on Adam and Even [*sic*] in Eden combined with Alice-in Wonderland and DP's[3] in general. The second uses the fairytale Oz yellow-brick road to take the place of Dante's road of life and the pilgrimage in Bunyan's book. The third plays on the inexorable black magic of time passing, childhood, dreams lost, and the final taste of inevitable death."

Qabalah, in all its spellings, which includes starting with a C or K, and ending with an A or an H, is the divine system on which all things operate. Call it God. Call it energy. Believe in it or don't. It doesn't matter if you acknowledge it; pretty soon you are going to

---

[3] "DPs" is a post-World War II expression for "displaced persons" when referring to refugees. It's important to notice that Plath cast Adam and Eve as refugees here, because she did it again, thematically, in "Lady Lazarus."

acknowledge that there are some amazing patterns running the show.

Qabalah is considered by its practitioners to be the law of the universe, and the Qabalah's Tree of Life is the blueprint for how it's built. When you read Plath's *Ariel* poems using your *Decoding* toolkit, it is important to see how these mirrors work together to reflect the same greater idea. We see this use of Qabalah's symbols and organization across the literary work of the greats, such as Dante, Chaucer, Milton, and Shakespeare, and more recently in the work of Yeats, Plath and Ted Hughes. Whether the word is familiar to you or not, Qabalah is everywhere: The world-famous, prolific author Hermann Hesse illustrated the Qabalah's Tree of Life in his novel *Magister Ludi*, also known as *The Glass Bead Game*. Tarot, meanwhile, has crept into poetry (think of T.S. Eliot's *The Waste Land*), and fiction (Umberto Eco's *Foucault's Pendulum* or Thomas Pynchon's *Gravity's Rainbow*, for just a few 20th-century examples). Hollywood movies use, or at least romanticize, the tarot. Many of us saw the Death card for the first time in the James Bond flick *Live and Let Die*. The cards show up in *Ocean's Twelve* and even *Supergirl*. Even on television, they've guested on *Mad Men, Xena: the Warrior Princess*, and *The Simpsons*. So, Qabalah is the lesser-known, omnipresent force that rules regardless of whether or not we want to acknowledge it. Tarot, Qabalah's trusty sidekick and modern-age wingman, is one of its languages and has been a part of human culture for hundreds of years. Traditional practitioners of Qabalah, which began as ancient Jewish mysticism, believe that Kabbalah with a K, the Jewish brand, pre-dates world religions. You might also think of Qabalah as being the greatest of poems: it is meant to be interpreted literally, allegorically, through language with imaginative comparisons of similar words and verses, and also metaphysically. No wonder Plath and Hughes were drawn to it. Consider this quote from the Zohar, the principle Qabalistic text:

> "The Zohar discusses the universe, as a whole, in far broader terms than merely the physical universe. Indeed, the physical

universe, as vast as it may be, is dwarfed in comparison with the mystical universe that embraces angelic and demonic realms. Whereas the physical universe is measured in time and distance, the mystical universe is measured in terms of levels of awareness. These levels should not be viewed as separate boundaries, for awareness is a continuum."

Did I lose you? That's okay. Just know that the last statement, about awareness being a continuum, means that everything you know is understood because it connects to something else. That's enough for now.

The Qabalah's Tree of Life is a kind of roadmap to self-actualization and owning your God-power. We know for sure that Plath knew a great deal about Qabalah, the Zohar, and the Tree of Life from the books in her library, many of which are listed in the Bibliography of this book. It is all in there in great deal, along with other occult practices written of in FSGL. In Plath's poem "The Munich Mannequins" she names it outright: "The tree of life and the tree of life," and further in the poem, she describes how this tree appears in its assembly: "Orange lollies on silver sticks."

You will see a lot of the word "mirrors" in *Fixed Stars Govern a Life,* in this book, and in other *Decoding* books. In *Kabbalah and Criticism*, author Harold Bloom says the stations of Kabbalah are "sometimes imaged as a mirror, in which God enjoys contemplating himself." Think of the mirrors I present here as the angled kind you see when trying on clothes in a department store. It is the same body, the same story, told or viewed from different perspectives. That's what Plath has done in her *Ariel* poems.

Why Would Plath Hide The Occult?

What's the big deal about keeping all this stuff secret? There are plenty of reasons, starting with the fact that witchcraft had only just been taken off the books as a crime in England a few years before Plath arrived. Add to this the facts that she had a history of mental illness and would have risked being called "crazy"; she might have jeopardized her serious career in a then-uptight and conservative academic world and her publishing pursuits in respected publications; and her young children she wanted to protect from gossip and harm. Put yourself in her shoes. These are reasons aplenty.

The Connection Between Plath and Tarot

It's important to remember that Sylvia Plath had a great interest in tarot cards, Taroc (a game using tarot cards), and other forms of mysticism. She owned a tarot deck and books on tarot, mysticism and the occult. Since her childhood, in fact, the game Taroc was a regular part of her life and family heritage. Even her psychiatrist used tarot cards with Plath as a young adult, to open up her consciousness to her deeper feelings and understanding. Remember also that every *Ariel* poem matches a tarot card, which fits on the Qabalah's Tree of Life. You can see that Plath names Taroc in her poem Daddy."

But, wait! Sylvia Plath didn't believe in God...

Maybe you've heard or read that Plath was an atheist. It is true that she did not believe that God was a man in the sky, but she was intensely spiritual. The evidence is plentiful: She regularly attended her Unitarian Universalist church as a girl, what we would call a spiritual or even a New Age church today, without being religious. Unitarian Universalism is a liberal religion with wide-ranging beliefs including atheism, agnosticism, pantheism, deism, Judaism, Islam, Christianity, neopaganism, Hinduism, Buddhism, Taoism, Humanism and more. Plath's diary notes mention her homework for Sunday school, on the astrological zodiac. She carved an alchemical caduceus out of wood in high school, and she immersed herself in mythology, drawing pictures of Greek gods and goddesses. Her honors thesis included Jungian archetypes and alchemical symbolism. We know that as an adult, Plath was passionate about and regularly practiced tarot, astrology, crystal ball reading, Ouija boards, she set witchy bonfires, and more. In journals and letters, Plath and Hughes mailed out their submissions for contests and publication based on auspicious dates dictated by the stars. Hughes taught Plath meditation techniques and hypnotized her regularly, and the two were condemned by the local reverend as "educated pagans." In 1999, A. Alvarez, ex-poetry editor of *The Observer* and close friend of Plath and her husband, even wrote an article for *The Guardian* called "How Black Magic Killed Sylvia Plath." Fairly or unfairly, the occult is where Alvarez put the blame.

Oh, that occult stuff creeps me out, I hear you saying. You don't have to practice any form of the occult to understand that the spell Plath puts upon us in her poem "Lady Lazarus" is powerful. You won't have to cross any boundaries you're uncomfortable with, and you don't even have to learn much about it. However, by the end of this book, you will be changed in the way you view this poem and Plath herself.

About Plath's "Jew" References

A lot of critics and readers have given Plath trouble for comparing herself to Holocaust victims in World War II. On the surface, it does look as if that is what she's doing. What nerve, right? She had white privilege and never suffered such racial or cultural persecution. But with a bit of background about tarot and Qabalah, you will soon know there is a whole lot more going on. Inaccurate dates and exaggerated claims were not merely her uses of poetic license. These are references to Qabalah. Now that you know that much, Plath's Jewish references should make much more sense:

- Qabalah, originally Kabbalah, is a form of ancient Jewish mysticism.
- The Hebrew language is considered mystical in and of itself, with numerical values assigned to each letter. Jews and

Kabbalists believe that the Hebrew language has a divine origin and supernatural power, and the letters illustrate the process of God creating the world.
- The Qabalah's Tree of Life positions each of the 22 Hebrew letters on their stations and paths.
- The tarot's major arcana has 22 cards, reflecting these Hebrew letters and Qabalah positions.

Oh, and should you question it, Plath had loads of books on religion and topics of Judaism in particular in her personal library.

"I began to talk like a Jew. / I think I may well be a Jew."
—Sylvia Plath, from her poem "Daddy."

Lilith, the Fiery Goddess

Let's talk about the focus of this book, Plath's poem, "Lady Lazarus," and what it has to do with tarot and Qabalah. As the seventh poem in *Ariel,* this matches The Lovers tarot card, which is the seventh station on the Tree of Life. Because the numbers on these cards begin with zero, The Lovers card is labeled number *six.* Don't let that confuse you. The Lovers is a card of balance between the conscious and the subconscious mind, as well as the sacred and the profane. The meaning of this card is less about romance and more about choice and the lethal passions that often do us in. The Lovers card is at odds with itself, battling to live or die, to be darkness or light. It can represent communion or discord. The Lovers has time only for itself and gives or receives no attention to or from others outside the relationship (like a really obsessive romance). After all, attention from others, as in "Lady Lazarus," is just scrutiny. The Lovers won't be a circus act to entertain "the peanut-crunching crowd."

The Lovers card features a picture of a fiery angel calling to Adam and Eve in the Garden of Eden. If you've never seen a picture of this card, get online and look it up to get a sense of the beautiful colors and scene. The three figures in the picture represent the conscious mind (male), the subconscious mind (female), and the higher self (the angel, or Cupid in an older tarot deck, the Tarot de Marseilles). The Lovers is a card of opposites and attraction: the active against the passive, light to dark, conscious to unconscious, and positive to negative. Like the Taoists' yin-yang, if you know that popular symbol.

Some tarot scholars say that it is not Eve pictured with Adam on The Lovers card, but Lilith, who was, technically, the first woman created by God. Lilith misbehaved by refusing to lie beneath a man. Lilith wanted equality, and in that old-fashioned man's world, she got kicked out of the garden. Plath knew all about Lilith, as she was a great reader of mythology and we know for sure that she owned several books which tell this story. Plath knew her personal struggles as a woman, and that even with the right to vote, women of her day were still considered second-class citizens. For instance, when she arrived in London in 1956, she was not allowed to walk around town unescorted by a man after dusk, and she was forbidden to enter certain bars, nightclubs, and restaurants without a male escort. She wrote:

> "Being born a woman is my awful tragedy. From the moment I was conceived I was doomed to sprout breasts and ovaries rather than penis and scrotum; to have my whole circle of action, thought and feeling rigidly circumscribed by my inescapable feminity [sic]. Yes, my consuming desire to mingle with road crews, sailors and soldiers, bar room regulars - to be a part of scene, anonomous [sic], listening, recording - all is spoiled by the fact that I am a girl, a female always in danger of assault and battery. My consuming interest in men and their lives is often misconstrued as a desire to seduce them, or as an invitation to intimacy. Yet, God, I want to talk to everybody I can as deeply as I can. I want to be able to sleep in an open field, to travel west, to walk freely at night ..."

This behavior she yearned for was inappropriate for a young woman in 1956 London. Plath's Lilith-like desire for feminine equality takes on more importance as we go on.

You are about to see, in "Lady Lazarus," that Plath is a little more Lilith than Eve. She does not submit to the male-dominant paradigm, not at all. Plath creates a fictional self that speaks freely and is insubordinate and even rebellious in the cultural climate imposed upon the early-1960s housewife she had become.

Plath learned to read her tarot cards from *The Painted Caravan,* what she called "my favorite book," by Basil Ivan Rákóczi. About the book, she said:

> "I have the queerest love for holding it, staring at the pictures; read the introduction in which the author claims the Gypsies have incorporated all the ritualistic rites of all religions and cults in their Tarot pack (a sort of World-Book) and that the Initiate can penetrate beyond the surface denotative meaning of the symbols, through the veils, etc. to the Alone. I meditated on the Fool and the Juggler, staring at the pictures, reading and re-reading the lucid, pleasantly written descriptions of them and their significance. I shall go through the whole book slowly this way, so that I shall come upon the difficulties of setting out the Pack with a basic sense, at least, of the cards, which will flow and re-cross and blend, I think, by great concentration and much practice. I really look forward to giving this my deepest love and attention; I feel very 'kin" to the cards, sort of."

In this book, the definition for The Lovers card is one who passes "through all manner of tests and trials, both of his physical and mental strength." If you're already familiar with the "Lady Lazarus" poem, you have begun to see some of this description within its words. If you're new to the poem, watch for these images.

Does it matter which tarot deck I'm looking at?

How do I know I'm looking at the deck Plath used?

Sylvia Plath most likely used a deck called the Rider-Waite Tarot, which was most commonly available in 1950s England (they didn't have the huge assortment of decks we have available today). She had a book in her personal library by the creator of this tarot deck, Arthur Waite. Plath's *Ariel* poems' matching with the Rider-Waite Tarot artwork supports that she probably owned this deck.

During the Renaissance age, a different tarot deck was used across Europe: the Tarot de Marseilles. Then, a little more than a hundred years ago, an occult organization emerged in Great Britain called The Hermetic Order of the Golden Dawn. In those Victorian times, spiritualism was all the rage, especially among the more subversive types, and artists and writers including William Butler Yeats joined the Golden Dawn and practiced their incantations, alchemy, and word-spells hidden behind the veil of their literary craft. Plath loved Yeats, by the way. She even moved into his former flat in London, an impulse she confirmed through bibliomancy, which is the occult practice of letting a random passage in a book guide your decision-making. Anyway, The Golden Dawn, to which Yeats and his friends belonged, created the modern Rider-Waite Tarot deck. It is based on the Tarot de Marseilles but adapted to better fit the Qabalah.

The Golden Dawn links a Hebrew letter to The Lovers card: *Zain*, meaning: "the sword of discrimination and the sword wielded by the hand of the faithful and zealous." The Hebrew language has a numeric correlation to all of its letters and words, and this card's number means that the ego must undergo total death before resurrection.

Death! Resurrection! You are starting to see how this matches "Lady Lazarus," but we have only begun to scratch the surface.

Where is The Lovers card in "Lady Lazarus"? This poem doesn't seem like a love story!

In the tarot, The Lovers is not necessarily about love at all. It is a card of choice, complementary forces, and a battle between the sacred and superficial things of the world. It holds the same thrill or "charge" of excitement that Plath gives the reader in the nineteenth stanza of "Lady Lazarus." When a tarot card reader interprets this card right-side up, The Lovers usually means union; reversed, it is a split.

When Plath marks one of every ten years in "Lady Lazarus," this also has tarot and qabalistic significance. While ten is not attached to The Lovers as the seventh card, the number ten is a milestone, as completion of a cycle. We saw that same importance in the twelfth stanza:

"The first time it happened I was ten."

You see, the first lines of "Lady Lazarus" mention the repetition of this cycle of tens. Another book known to be written on qabalistic patterns and theories, James Joyce's *Finnegans Wake*,[4] echoes this. In a book Plath owned and read, *A Skeleton Key to Finnegans Wake* by Joseph Campbell, the author explains the numerical importance, "the old decade having run out with ten," emphasizing this as a number of great change in Qabalah. *Finnegans Wake* was a book important enough to Plath that she studied it for her thesis and bought Campbell's book to understand it better. Joyce used a technique of multiple references, or saying the same thing many different ways. This is exactly what Plath did

---

[4] For more on James Joyce's *Finnegans Wake*, see my book in this series, *Decoding Sylvia Plath's "Daddy."*

in her *Ariel* poems, and her underlinings and annotations in *The Portable James Joyce* support this.

In "Lady Lazarus," Plath's poetic decision reflects The Lovers' meaning of making a choice: whether to live or die. The Lovers card is the occult initiation into a new life, as two become one. It is also the art of killing the old singular life. It will soon become a perfect metaphor for the immigrant, which we will see more about later in this book.

Judging from the books in her library[5] and her husband's extensive anthropological and metaphysical pursuits, we can be reasonably sure that Plath knew that in earlier times, Qabalah was forbidden to women and non-Jews. In fact, it was said that no one under the age of forty should delve into its secrets without risking insanity. (Are you thinking what I am thinking? A believer might think Plath went too far with it.) As a non-Jewish woman and declaring her age of thirty[6] in the poem, Plath defiantly peeled off the napkin-veil hiding her fiery feminine power. Like Lilith, she wasn't about to be told what she could or could not do as a woman.

"Lady Lazarus" and The Lovers card both embody a battle and a choice between wanting to live or die: an occult initiation into new life and the art of killing the old one. Think of Plath's words now: "Dying is an art." The choice to be made is a conflicting one, and so The Lovers card also represents loss, because to choose one thing is to give up another, as we see in the nineteenth stanza of "Lady Lazarus."

Remember the old Bible story about the raising of Lazarus? If you don't know it, the story goes that there were these religious leaders, the Pharisees, regarded as representatives of the Old Mysteries. A man named Lazarus had been dead for a few days, and it was certainly considered a hopeless case for the guy to recover.

---

[5] Plath owned *The Unicorn: William Butler Yeats' Search For Reality* by Virginia Moore, as well as many books on Mormonism, which explain Qabalah (spelled Kabbalah in some of these books) and alchemy in great detail.
[6] Plath acknowledges being underage for this practice again in the following poem, "Tulips."

Yet Jesus came around and resurrected him three days dead. Lazarus went on to live a long and healthy second life. The Pharisees, meanwhile, considered Lazarus's raising a betrayal and violation of ancient tradition. Jesus had disregarded the old ways. The times they were a-changin', and this miraculous act which was kept as an occult secret had now gone public. Similarly, this is what Plath did. In her *Ariel* poems and "Lady Lazarus" especially, this is "The big strip tease," and she is dropping not clothes, but ego, flesh, and bone. To take the metaphor even further, it resembles what we're doing here, uncovering this whole decoding process.

Hughes wrote about the *Ariel* poems:

> "So it seems very clear, for instance, that as she moved towards the liberation of her real voice, she moved towards the liberation of her child self, which was actually in the grave with her dead father. When she liberated her dead father which was also her real/her child self in the grave, she raised her own death."

Cupid is the angel pictured on The Lovers card of the Tarot de Marseilles, the deck that inspired the Rider-Waite Tarot. Cupid was a mischievous, winged child who taunted humans, firing his gold-tipped arrows of desire. Cupid is a great pictorial representation of Plath's words "pure gold baby" ...and we haven't even started to talk about alchemy yet (that's coming up).

Qabalists believe that female energy is separated from the attributes of God by sin. It's the Judeo-Christian Adam and Eve story once again, and outside of ancient goddess-worshipping civilizations, most of human history has reflected this belief. Because of this separation, female energy was exiled to the *Qliphoth*, the dark side of the Tree of Life, which is explained in Plath's book on Yeats, *The Unicorn: William Butler Yeats' Search for Reality*. Hermeticists believe the Qliphoth holds "The Seven Infernal Habitations," or seven hells, strengthening "Lady Lazarus" as the seventh poem with this seventh tarot card (remember that we start the count with zero in the tarot's Major Arcana). Translated, Qliphoth means "peel" or "shells." So now you have a new understanding of the napkin Plath peels off in the fourth stanza and the shells of the peanut-crunchers in her ninth stanza. Think of Plath's poems as they relate one to the other as you read this quotation:

> "God saw that it was necessary to put into the world so as to make sure of permanence all things having, so to speak, a brain surrounded by numerous membranes. The whole world, upper and lower, is organized on this principle, from the primary mystic center to the very outermost of all the layers. All are coverings, the one to the other, brain within brain, spirit inside of spirit, shell within shell."
> —from The Zohar (the most important book of the Qabalah)

The feminine fire is said to be imprisoned within the Qliphoth hells. That's *hells*, not shells. One of the hells is called *Golachab*. Personified as a woman, Golachab destroys the wicked and fights evil and injustice, maintaining equilibrium with her positive side of loving kindness. Golachab's weapon of destruction is fire, and she sometimes burns everything down, including—oops!—what should not be burned. This fire is probably an old sexist metaphor for a woman's temper, but, whatever. In *Kabbalah and Criticism*, author Harold Bloom writes, "Kabbalah is nothing if not sexist."

There *is* something good to be said about women in Qabalah, however: Qabalists believe that only through love can the feminine energy be freed to transform the Earth spiritually. Pure ego, a masculine trait, will recombine at a higher level to reactivate the *Sophia*, the female mythological personification of wisdom and the feminine expression of God.

Now you've got the fundamentals down. Let's move on to the juicy stuff!

CHAPTER FOUR

Second Mirror: Alchemy

The Alchemical Marriage of The Lovers

"When Ted and I begin living together we shall become a team better than Mr. and Mrs. Yeats—he being a competent astrologist, reading horoscopes, and me being a tarot-pack reader, and, when we have enough money, a crystal-gazer."
—Sylvia Plath, in a letter to her mother, October 28, 1956

Alchemy! Where do we start? It sounds very close to chemistry, which probably has many of you running the other way. It did me too, at first. And chemistry is a part of it. But before your eyes glaze over and you fall asleep at your desk, understand that alchemy is actually a pretty sexy topic. I mean that literally, as alchemy is full of sexual metaphor because it's about uniting opposites to create something new. Sexually, that is a man and a woman joining bodies to make a child. Spiritually, it is bringing the physical and the emotional together to achieve the divine. And in practical chemistry, it's about making gold. You might have heard that the alchemists of medieval times strove to turn lead into gold. Some of them even claim to have succeeded (If that's true, they hid their evidence well). It was believed that civilizations could be created and destroyed with this knowledge. These mystical practitioners wrote their alchemical secrets in coded language, to keep it within a select group of the spiritually pure so that it would be used for good and not for evil. In a *Smithsonian* magazine article, an alchemical text describes a chemical as a "cold dragon" that "creeps in and out of the caves," for instance. These metaphors made sense, as they were actually writing about the chemical potassium nitrate, or saltpeter, a cool, crystalline substance found on cave walls. So it's not as nonsensical as it seems at the first impression. Some of the secret societies which practiced (and might still practice) alchemy are the Freemasons, the Rosicrucians, and the Illuminati. Oh yes, and we see loads of it in Harry Potter.

For more than 2000 years, we've seen alchemy in medicine, the arts and humanities, and in religions practiced by people across Europe, the Middle East, and Asia. Alchemy is not a failed science, as many people tend to believe. It isn't a religion or magic, either. Rather, it is the ancient tradition of striving to turn the ordinary into the extraordinary. Sir Isaac Newton, a historical genius whom we still respect, was a full-on alchemist. The first and most famous alchemist is a guy named Paracelsus, who happened to be the subject of the thesis Aurelia Plath wrote for her Master of Arts degree from Boston University. Aurelia is the mother of Sylvia Plath, so as you can see, the alchemical acorn did not fall far from the Qabalah's Tree. Plath also owned books such as *The Unicorn*, which discusses alchemy in all the specifics I'll soon be mentioning. From this book, the biographer sums up Yeats's take on alchemy (which he practiced through Rosicrucianism), his regular practices, and nearly every strange term you will read in this book shows up there.

Alchemy, like its buddy Qabalah, can be pursued through different means. There is practical alchemy which is chemistry in the lab, concerned with turning lead to gold. That's the alchemy I am sure you have already heard about. Next, there is psychological alchemy around emotional development and concerned with turning a base, primitive person into a successful and happy contributor to society. And finally, there is spiritual alchemy, about becoming so pure as to be one with God.

Years even before Plath met Hughes, she pondered this idea:

> "... Frustrated? Yes. Why? Because it is impossible for me to be God - or the universal woman-and-man - or anything much. I am what I feel and think and do. I want to express my being as fully as I can because I somewhere picked up the idea that I could justify my being alive that way. But if I am to express what I am, I must have a standard of life, a jumping-off place, a technique - to make arbitrary and temporary organization of my own personal and pathetic little chaos. I am just beginning to realize how false and provincial that standard, or jumping-off place, must be. That is what is so hard for me to face."

Plath's endeavors into the occult world were the technique she was looking for. The true alchemist works on every level. You've probably been striving to alchemize yourself in the emotional realm, and you didn't even know it: You graduated from grade school and perhaps went to college to find a life imbued with purpose, passion and spiritual meaning. Psychologist Carl Jung, a student of Sigmund Freud's, developed his own brand of alchemy, known as Jungian alchemy. Jungian alchemy strives toward self-actualization and reaching one's highest potential. There are seven stages in alchemy (remember that The Lovers card is the seventh station, and "Lady Lazarus" is the seventh poem).

Like the monks who still practice alchemy today in Thailand and Burma, the alchemical beginner, or Initiate, seeks to separate from the world and develop his or her senses of perception to great heights. That means developing all kinds of perception, beyond the five senses. For the alchemist, the world and the physical body mean nothing; they merely encase the spirit.

While some thesis papers have touched on alchemy in Plath's work, for the most part, this subject has been missed or pooh-

poohed by academia. Most people don't know squat about alchemy. Can you really blame them? It all sounds super-weird, and academics are specialists in education and literature, but not necessarily historians or psychologists, or even artists. They might know about art, what they have been told, but they do not specialize in understanding the creative process. About this subject, Sylvia Plath said in her June 11, 1958 journal entry:

> "The horror of the academic writer is that he lives on air and other people's second-hand accounts of other people's writing…"

Plath mirrors the alchemical separation in "Lady Lazarus" with her Nazi-like perception of the human body: flesh can be used to make household objects, in her second and third stanzas. The first four stanzas in "Lady Lazarus" present a Josef Mengele-ish alchemical madman ("Herr Doktor"), transmuting the human body not into a higher spirit, but to the mundane: lampshades, paperweights, and linens.

Plath's "paperweight" might refer to important alchemical texts such as the "Stockholm Papyrus." Regardless of what paper is weighted, alchemy uses terms such as "laundering" and even "women's work" and "child's play" in the transmutation of metals. Plath's use of the word "linen" is a term for the White Stage in alchemy, cleansing impurities and regenerating and transforming matter. To read some of these old alchemical text directions sounds much like the drudging duties of a housewife. Nevertheless, a sense of transformation certainly concludes this poem.

In the New Testament's Book of John, 11:44, the biblical Lazarus's face was bound with a napkin that Jesus commands be removed. Plath commands her enemy to do the same, to reveal the truth of her. In the Bible, that napkin is a metaphor of the limited, blind, and even a dead world view of hopelessness. Alchemical consciousness believes in moving beyond the limitations of our current reality, the rational mind, linear time, and the material world. We see Plath move through all these realities in "Lady Lazarus" too.

Think about it: We're using a transformative alchemical consciousness all the time, and we don't realize it. It shifts our belief system when we believe something formerly impossible is possible. For instance, even only fifty years ago, in Plath's time, Olympic athletes never dreamed of running or swimming or jumping with as much speed as our athletes can today. They would have said the world records set in our time were impossible. To make a thing possible, we must first imagine it. To declare it can't be done, or to say that it is impossible, makes it so—impossible for the one declaring it, that is. In "Lady Lazarus," Plath imagines her power before she has it, before the world has seen it. And we can be sure that she attained what she visualized, even if her success mostly came posthumously.

The features of the face in Plath's fifth stanza of "Lady Lazarus" are also aspects of the alchemical process. In the alchemical lab, alchemists use items called alembic glassware. All of these details of the practice and materials are throughout *The Unicorn*, Plath's book on Yeats, as it discusses Yeats's adventures in alchemy in search of his own Philosopher's Stone

One part of the alembic glassware is called a *nose*. There are eyes in alchemy too: *fishes' eyes*, to be exact. *Fishes' eyes* is the label used when the stone has reached the state of whitening and takes on an undeniable iridescence comparable to pearls or "teeth." Nose, eyes, pearls, and teeth are all named clearly in "Lady Lazarus." Plath's image of bad breath in this same stanza is the foul smell during the chemical stage of putrefaction, also known as the Black Phase. The "grave cave" of "Lady Lazarus" is the alchemist's alembic vessel during the Black Phase, known as (surprise!) *the grave*. All impure matter burns and disintegrates there. Are you getting excited yet? As you're learning, we don't have to be scholars of alchemy to see Plath's tricks.

Maybe you were also astute enough to notice that the mystical, magical cat creeps into Plath's work every so often. In the *Ariel* collection, we see the cat mentioned in "Morning Song," "Lady Lazarus," "Tulips," "The Jailor," and "The Other." Kittens appear in "Lesbos," lionesses are in the title poem "Ariel" and in "Purdah," and we see "her lion-red body" in "Stings." Every feline in Plath's poetry is gender-neutral, or else the cat is female. Alchemy often uses the symbol of a female lion (usually red or green). You will see that Plath's cat simile in the seventh stanza corresponds to this. In alchemy, all four elements must be "killed" nine times, like a cat's proverbial nine lives, to get to the tenth new cycle.

Plath's idea of "trash" refers to the waste, or dross, left by alchemical work. "A million filaments"[7] are the repeated burnings during this process. The old ways no longer work in a new, changed form as Plath annihilates her past decades in the eighth stanza.

In "Lady Lazarus," if you read it literally, Plath claims to have been near to death three times in her life: in an accident as a ten-year-old child[8]; from intentionally taking too many sleeping pills at twenty; and, as A. Alvarez wrote in *Sylvia Plath: A Memoir*:

> "...about her recent incident with the car. It had been no accident; she had gone off the road deliberately, seriously, wanting to die. But she hadn't, and all that was now in the past. For this reason, I am convinced that at this time she was not contemplating suicide. On the contrary, she was able to write about the act so freely because it was already behind her. The car crash was a death she had survived, the death she sardonically felt herself fated to undergo once every decade."

If you close your eyes and listen to Plath's great audio recording of "Lady Lazarus," (something you ought to do), you might imagine Plath stepping out of her emotion to witness the horrors of death as an impersonal circus sideshow or exhibit. Voyeurs of peanut-eating

---

[7] See the discussion of "million" in the *Fixed Stars Govern a Life* interpretation of Sylvia Plath's poem, "Cut."
[8] While Plath claims nearing death at ten years old in the poem "Lady Lazarus," this has never been verified.

spectators circle her nakedness. However, surveying this scene through alchemical lenses presents a different view: These lines represent the dross or earthy remains left at the bottom of the vessel. They are useless and dry, like empty peanut shells after the nut has been lifted out. The alchemist unwraps his stone from these outside layers in a process called Ablution. This is a precursor to the White Phase of rebirth.

Plath seemed to like the word "nevertheless," also using it twice in her poem "Medusa." The idea of rebirth correlates with Plath's line, "Nevertheless, I am the same, identical woman." How? Let me show you: "Nevertheless" is more than a conjunctive adverb in these poems. The word echoes that idea of being equivalent to or greater than, but never less. In her use of this single word, Plath expands the feminist elements featured in other mirrors of "Lady Lazarus," soon to be revealed. Also, check out the comma after "same." Plath has not changed who she is, and yet she looks at a mirror image. Her "[S]ame" and "identical" is no careless redundancy. It is the alchemy of ascending from her earthly form ("nevertheless" now means *not-less-than*) to spiritual formlessness (becoming the "same," because everyone is one on the other side), and then descending back into the original form as a forever-changed being yet still herself (the "identical woman").

You remember, of course, that The Lovers tarot card, associated with "Lady Lazarus," pictures a naked couple. We might think of those lovers as being in front of an audience (ourselves, as we look at the card). There is the nakedness in Plath's tenth and eleventh stanzas of the poem.

A part of this poem deleted from an earlier draft but preserved in the recorded version also mentions the Japanese. In World War II, the Japanese were firebombed for six months, followed by the dropping of atom bombs on Hiroshima and Nagasaki: World War II Japan is the ultimate alchemical metaphor for the Black phase of fire before rebirth.[9]

When Plath "rocked" shut in stanza thirteen, this is the closed Black phase of the *philosopher's stone*. I know that most of you have heard that phrase "philosopher's stone" in Harry Potter books. Sometimes the philosopher's stone is called the *philosopher's child*, and sometimes it's called gold (remember: alchemy is baseness to purity, or lead to gold). Whichever way you choose to view it, Plath ties the word *pure* to describe a baby here, as well as in her poems "Getting There" and "A Birthday Present." This is not the purity of innocence we're talking about. This is pure as in "free of chemical contamination" like the old Ivory Soap slogan that claimed the soap was "99.44 percent pure." And look later on in *Ariel,* in "Fever 103°" when she writes, "I am too pure for you or anyone" and "I, / Am a pure acetylene / Virgin." There is power in alchemical purity after burning.

The seashell image in "Lady Lazarus" is from the Mother Sea, the mercurial waters or primal material from which Venus the mother rises, and everything is made. Venus is said to rise from sea foam and called the "deep-sea daughter" in *Finnegans Wake*.

Then there's decomposition. Physical decomposition is an important stage in the complete alchemical union. Where do you see decomposition in "Lady Lazarus"? Worms are synonymous in alchemy with the serpent and the dragon symbols. They devour the old, corrupt body, simultaneously giving life to the infant stone. When the stone reaches the White phase, its "teeth" take on the glittering opalescence of "pearls."

Plath's art of dying in the fifteenth stanza sums up alchemical transmutation; the old form is killed for the new one, the *opus magnum* to be born. It's no accident when Plath says, "I am your opus" in "Lady Lazarus." We'll talk about that in a second.

For the moment, let's look at the idea of the cell in the seventeenth stanza. This choice of words for Plath could reference the cells of matter as much as a prison; whether or not it has this

---

[9] See *Fixed Stars Govern a Life*'s interpretation of "Ariel" for more about Japan and the bombings of Hiroshima and Nagasaki.

double meaning, "prison" is also an alchemical term for the vessel during the Black phase of *putrefaction* and *nigredo*. To "stay put," as Plath said it, is to be stuck in putrefaction when the stone is killed.

Alchemy and theater were closely associated in the 15th century. Shakespeare had countless alchemical references in his plays. Alchemical treatises were often entitled "theatres," as books to give "a view" or "conspectus" on a subject, another take on Plath's "theatrical / Comeback." Alchemists also regarded the alembic vessel as the theater in which a miniature creation imitated the creation of the greater world.[10]

The word "charge," in addition to meaning the price we pay for something and also a jolt of electricity, means duty and responsibility. Just look how Plath made her words work. It is mind-blowing. In Alchemy, a *charge* is this work that the alchemist takes on willingly. Famous alchemist George Ripley wrote of experimenting with hair and blood, among other substances. Plath's *word, touch, blood, hair,* and *clothes* are examples of physical matter left behind and are also full of Nazi allusions.

Now, let's get back to that word "opus." In alchemy, *magnum opus* is Latin for "Great Work"; it is the success of transforming lead into gold, creating the philosopher's stone, and it is a metaphor for spiritual transformation. In Rosicrucianism, it is the "Chemical Wedding," also apt for The Lovers tarot card which I'm sure you know by now corresponds to "Lady Lazarus." The famous alchemist Benjamin Lock wrote that the chemical wedding paradoxically takes place through strife, difficulty and opposing forces. A sacred marriage of male and female aspects is the goal; its initiation ritual is a procession of tests, purification, death, resurrection, and ascension—rising into the air. Sounds like a marriage made in heaven, right? It also sounds exactly like "Lady Lazarus."

---

[10] This miniature creation is the *homunculus*, mentioned by name in Plath's poem "Cut."

After the 15th century, alchemists considered that there were three stages in this initiation, correlating with Plath's eighth-stanza line: "This is Number Three." This third and last stage is called *Rubedo*, meaning a reddening, like the hair in the last stanza of "Lady Lazarus." Plath's own books tell us that red hair is actually a really big deal in mythology and ancient religions: The ancient Egyptians used to burn red-haired men alive and scatter their ashes as an offering to Osiris. Red-haired puppies were sacrificed in ancient Rome. Plath's image of red hair echoes the red *Herr*, meaning the unification of man or woman with God, and maybe challenging that red-haired *man* bit a little. And for those literalist sticklers, Plath did not have red hair.

Qabalists consider that when Jesus raised Lazarus in the New Testament, he acted as a Hierophant. A Hierophant is a priest who interprets and practices sacred mysteries. In "Lady Lazarus," Plath is her own Hierophant in the alchemical process of creating a higher self. The higher God-self is born through fire and tribulation. She is the pure gold-stone alchemical baby of the twenty-third stanza.

In the Biblical legend of Adam and Eve, associated with the picture on The Lovers card, Eve is tempted by fruits from the Tree of Knowledge. If you think about it, Eve was essentially the first alchemist, but in reverse: When Eve ate the forbidden fruit of wisdom, it elevated and separated her from the base animal kingdom. She turned away from God and into the burning, as in Plath's twenty-fourth stanza. In *A Skeleton Key to Finnegans Wake*, author Joseph Campbell says "The tree was the shrub of liberty." This liberty represents the Fall of Man in James Joyce's *Finnegans Wake*. Venus, Lucifer, the Fall of Man and the Garden of Eden are all through *Finnegans Wake*, which according to Campbell, was written to correspond with "Kabbala/Kabbalistic Theology." See, in the Fall of Man, the Biblical Eve becomes godlike in her ability to create life, yet with this choice, she also acquired the knowledge of physical death. Ouch. Like Adam and Eve, Plath sees contained within death the possibility of spiritual immortality. In this Bible story, we read: "And the Lord God said, 'The man has now become like one of us, knowing good and evil'" (Genesis: 3:22). Notice that God's pronoun is plural. Now, we know that Eve took the fruit first. Knowledge is power, but power has a price. Whether one is a man or a woman, becoming God is a pursuit for both sexes. This idea of becoming God is more important later on in this book.

In the twenty-fifth and twenty-sixth stanzas of "Lady Lazarus," Plath muses about being physically reduced to nothing but ash and bits of bone, the waxy soap of fat, and metal. At this point in "Lady Lazarus," her spirit, once of the Earth, has united with God. Ash remains after the alchemical phase of *Calcination*, a conversion of base metal to a fine white powder from heat. Ash will no longer support fire. Seen through the psychological metaphor of Jungian alchemy, she is free of passion, passion also being a characteristic of The Lovers card. Ash is synonymous with this White phase. Additionally, the "wedding ring" in "Lady Lazarus" correlates to the chemical wedding, and the "gold filling" may now mean filling oneself with or becoming gold. Whew! And there's more!

It's interesting that Plath uses German words in her poems, as she struggled to learn the language in school.[11] German is a notoriously paternalistic language, equating the woman with the word "It" in English.

The word *Herr* is German for "Lord," and the female counterpart of a Lord is a Lady, which takes us back to the title of the poem. The title of "Lord" identifies a prince, a feudal superior, a god or deity. The Hebrew name *YHWH* is rendered LORD. It is Hebrew practice not to speak or write God's true name. In true Lovers fashion, Plath has brilliantly united the idea of the healing "Herr Doktor" with his polar-opposite destroyer, "Herr Enemy," in the twenty-second stanza of "Lady Lazarus."

What does this have to do with alchemy? It correlates with alchemy's uniting of opposites: male and female, good and evil, all

---

[11] There is the amusing relic of her German textbook, stabbed multiple times with a knife or scissors, which can be found in the Sylvia Plath archives at Smith College.

represented by this Lovers card. Likewise, in her twenty-seventh stanza, she unites "Herr God" with "Herr Lucifer." Plath as a "Lady" rising from the dead equates with her polar opposite, Lord. She becomes the phoenix reborn; the philosopher's stone; an enlightened woman; a higher, more powerful creature than any mortal.

When Plath calls her hair red, she makes another common alchemical reference, in addition to the history of red heads we just saw. "Red head" is a symbol of the consummation of the opus; red is a property of copper and the goddess Venus, examined soon in other mirrors of this poem. Red is also the color of the *Rubedo* phase leading to pure gold. Finally, there is a famous alchemical drawing of the Green Lion, which is sometimes portrayed as female. In a well-known alchemical engraving, the green female lion devours the male Sun. Search the web for "Green Lion Devouring the Sun," and you'll see many pictures of this scene. Remembering that fiery red copper turns green from oxidation, this element also shares a symbol with the planet Venus, with the goddess Venus, and with the female sex in biology. It is clarification for the dynamic and unforgettable last line of "Lady Lazarus": "And I eat men like air."[12]

So now you've graduated from Alchemy 101. Congratulations!

---

[12] See footnote on eating oxygen in the *Fixed Stars Govern a Life: Decoding Sylvia Plath, Volume One* (2014, Stephen F. Austin State Press University) interpretation for Plath's poem, "Tulips."

CHAPTER SIX

Third Mirror: Mythology

I'm Your Venus, I'm Your Fire

> "Goddess on the mountain top
> Burning like a silver flame
> The summit of beauty and love
> And Venus was her name"
> —lyrics by the band Shocking Blue, 1969

Think back to when you were a small child in kindergarten. You gathered around in a circle for story time. Or maybe your parents read *Aesop's Fables* or *Grimms' Fairy Tales* to you as you snuggled in bed. These stories fascinated you with nuggets of wisdom in the guise of foxes and grapes, or enchanted snakes, or careless bulls outwitted by a sly lion. We know that stories are our best teachers. Since the philosopher Plato told his tales of the wise Socrates, our religious and political leaders, school professors, and even salespeople have learned that a good story is a way to hook interest and provide understanding. In *The White Goddess: a historical grammar of poetic myth* (an important book to Plath and Hughes), author Robert Graves claims mythology goes back to the Stone Age. We know since the Golden Age of ancient Greece that the authors of myths gave their gods human weaknesses, and their fictional humans occasionally had godlike powers, all in an attempt to explain the passions and mysteries of life. The famous German author Thomas Mann said:

> "Myth is the foundation of life; it is the timeless pattern, the religious formula to which life shapes itself…Whereas in the life of mankind the mythical represents an early and primitive stage, in the life of an individual it represents a late and mature one."

Plath knew that her German-Nordic ethnic background had myths associated with conquest, and also that the Nazis had attempted to reinstate the thought patterns of this earlier time, believing it was important to their cultural heritage. Plath's "Lady Lazarus" has mythology all over it, not only in the Bible story of Adam and Lilith and Eve that we saw two chapters ago, but also in the famous myth called "The Judgment of Paris."

Enter: The Lovers tarot card. This card is considered to be inspired by the mythological tale of "The Judgment of Paris," first recorded in writing in Homer's *Iliad*. Now you know why Paris, France is called the City of Love! The myth, about a young man, Paris, choosing between three goddesses, is a warning about passions running wild, and that the wrong choice will result in disastrous consequences. Yet we are suckers for passion. Everybody is! And these powerful, attractive forces cannot be ignored in Plath's church-mocking line in "Lady Lazarus": "I guess you could say I've a call."[13]

---

[13] See footnote on Carl G. Jung's "call" in the *Fixed Stars Govern a Life* interpretation of the poem, "The Jailor."

Meet Venus/Aphrodite

Venus/Aphrodite is our temptress, offering sexual delights. In the myth mentioned above, that young man Paris was required to choose between three goddesses: Hera, who held the riches of the world in her hand; Athene, who held power and victory in her sword; or Aphrodite, who offered the cup of love, with its pleasures of sex and sensuality.

As you probably have already guessed, Paris, a typical young man unable to suppress his libido, chose Aphrodite's sexual pleasures over riches or power, and he ultimately doomed his nation to war and lost his kingdom of Troy.

What chance did a mere mortal man have against the very fount of femininity? *The White Goddess* claims that these three women were not jealous rivals, but all aspects of the Triple Goddess, that complete expression of woman as maiden, mother, and crone first mentioned in our chapter on Connections.[14]

Where is The Judgment of Paris in "Lady Lazarus"? It's in the description and power of Venus. She represents themes of femininity, equality, and freedom. These ideas are all over this and other mirrors of the poem. For instance, Plath uses lots of little Venusian details in "Lady Lazarus." Let's start with Venus, the destroyer of men, as seen in Rosicrucianism.

The mythological founder of the Rosicrucians, Christian Rosenkreutz, legendarily wed the goddess Venus in the 15th-century work, *The Chymical Wedding of Christian Rosenkreutz*. In the story, Rosenkreutz, who was born in the 13th century, is said to have died and been reborn in 1378. Whether they're talking reincarnation or resurrection, the old alchemists took this story as literal fact. Rosenkreutz gave the world the slogan "Liberty, Equality, Fraternity" as watchwords to live by. These are ideas encompassing the Statue of Liberty, women's rights, and Freemasonry, which are all discussed in depth in the following

---

[14] This concept is well illustrated in Plath's verse play "Three Women."

mirrors of this poem. In a chapter of the Rosicrucian story called "The Fifth Day," it is written: "Here lies buried Lady Venus, the fair woman who hath undone many a great man." Plath certainly wrote "Lady Lazarus" with this male-conquering mindset.

Meet Lucifer/Isis

Remember back when Isis used to be the name of a really cool goddess, and not an acronym for a terrorist proto-state? Sigh.

One of the *cool* goddess Isis's symbols was the ankh, the Egyptian cross that represents resurrection. You have already seen the connection with the resurrection theme at the end of "Lady Lazarus" many times.

If you've read any of Plath's letters or journals, you might know that she related herself repeatedly to the Egyptian goddess Isis, as early as 1956, and even before she was with Ted Hughes. Later on, Hughes compared Plath to Isis too often to count. A framed print of an engraving of the goddess Isis hung over their fireplace in their Chalcot Square apartment in London, and later in their house in Devon. In this old print, a crowned Isis is pictured holding a ceremonial object in each hand, casting her magic as she stands upon the earth and sea.

What is the pattern here? Well, you won't be surprised to learn that Isis is *also* linked to the planet Venus. Isis is a counterpart of Venus/Aphrodite, and the Romans and Greeks both embraced Isis as their own. Because of these links, she is the equivalent of Lucifer, the brightest angel.

Wait. What?! Lucifer? But Lucifer is Satan…the devil!

I know, I know. That's what we've all been taught. The two are often confused, and it seems as if Plath had fun with that idea in her references to hell in "Lady Lazarus."

The name *Lucifer* shows up in only one place in the Bible, Isaiah 14:12, but this is only in the King James Versions. Here, and also in Ezekiel 28: 11-19 (where the King of Tyre represents Lucifer/Satan in the King James Versions), Lucifer ascends the Holy Mountain to become equal with God (Apparently, that was a *big* mistake ol' Lucifer made, which resulted in a permanent demotion to Hell). Lucifer in Latin means "light-bringer." In other translations which are more accurate than the King James Versions and closer to the original Hebrew, we see instead: "O shining star of the dawn!" or "O morning-star, son of the dawn!"

Before there was a New Testament of the Bible, there was Plato, thought to have been born in 428 BCE. Plato pre-dates the Bible as a collection, but the Torah predates Plato by a lot. The Hebrew Torah, which is pictured on the lap of The High Priestess card in the tarot, was composed and compiled around 1314 CE. Plath was a huge fan of Plato, with notes and observations so good that her Cambridge professor expanded her lessons from Plath's work.

In his dialogue called *Timaeus,* Plato specifically refers to the planet Venus as "Phosphorus." The evening star was known as "Hesperus" because the Greeks had not yet learned that the morning and evening star were the same planet. Plato suggests Hesperus is of the male gender, Phosphorus is female, and they "overtake and are overtaken by each other." But Plath read that Plato said Venus was Lucifer, because she had the translation by Benjamin Jowett. Benjamin Jowett[15] called Plato's "Phosphorus" "Lucifer," which is a Vulgate Latin spin on the original Hebrew "morning star," now recognized as a mistake. Yet *this spin* is what Plath and countless others read. Thus, Lucifer and Venus were linked, and because Lucifer was fallen and evil, Venus was tainted, while the planets with the male names were not.

An angel is said to be genderless, which is an interesting statement about sexual equality all by itself. Angels are also said to have free will, but not freedom of choice, which is a property of The

---

[15] Benjamin Jowett (1817-1893), an influential tutor and scholar at University of Oxford, England. Jowett is best-known for his translations of Plato and Thucydides. He has been labeled a heretical controversialist for his radical thoughts on women and politics, and his departure from liberal Anglican theology.

Lovers card. The Latin Vulgate Bible, which became the Catholic Church's doctrine, says that Lucifer is a great and powerful angel, as beautiful and bright as a star, like that planet Venus. According to legend, Lucifer's downfall came when it wanted equality with God. Rather like Lilith, eh? By contrast, Satan was never an angel. He was created to tempt mankind. As this tempter, Satan provides an opportunity for man to overcome hardships through faith.

In *The White Goddess*, author Robert Graves tells the story of The Son, Lucifer, a.k.a. Phosphorus, which means "bringer of light." Graves calls Lucifer the evening star, the planet Venus, born to the goddess every year, to grow up, destroy the serpent and then win the goddess's love. Yes, there is definitely a creepy Oedipal thing going on there, but we won't get into that.

From "Lady Lazarus," Plath's "Comeback in broad day" is the parallel. The goddess would destroy the son, and from his ashes, another serpent was born that laid a red egg. The goddess ate the red egg, and her son (the Sun) would be reborn to her. Her absolute power was celebrated as "Lady of the Wild Things," and societies worshipped her by burning their totem beasts alive. See it now? The ash, the red, the consuming of men, the Lady, and the burning of "Lady Lazarus" are there yet again.

Meet the First Females: Lilith and Eve

So, because Satan and Lilith wanted equality, and because Satan was created to tempt man, Lilith and Eve were created to do the same. It's the "same, identical" story, over and over, switching the names of the characters. That is how most mythology goes. And now you see how mythology, in a roundabout way, has also been interpreted by masculine-led cultures to judge and demonize women. In fact, even the symbol of the fruit used in the Genesis story—traditionally but not biblically said to be an apple—is a subtle criticism against women. If you slice an apple in half from stem to base, the pattern of the core and seeds resembles female genitalia. Try it and see. There were, of course, no apple trees in the Middle East; those who identified the fruit as an apple needed a good female metaphor to represent evil temptation. The female body, historically, is the ultimate sin and temptation for heterosexual males. But I digress.

Finally, the poem "Lady Lazarus" celebrates the mythological Lilith, who we met at the beginning of this book in the first mirror. We see her in both Jewish mythology and the Babylonian Talmud. As the first woman created for Adam in the Garden of Eden, she and Adam immediately began to fight. "I will not lie below," she said, and really, can you blame her? Adam told Lilith he would not lie beneath her either because he believed he was superior. Lilith responded that since they were both created from the earth, they were equals. Adam wouldn't listen, Lilith blasphemed God's name, and then Lilith rose into the air as Plath's "Lady Lazarus" rises, and abandoned Adam altogether.

In *A Skeleton Key to Finnegans Wake*, Campbell writes of Eve, "Listen to the mocking temptress." Certainly Plath does a bit of sarcastic mocking in "Lady Lazarus." This same book equates Eve with Isis. But as you're figuring out, they're all the same.

Meet Hecate/Brigit/Hera

In all this talk of death-and-rebirth, the three-fold goddess leads almost every mythology. Greeks and Romans called the triplicate goddess Hecate, goddess of moons, magic, necromancy, birth, witchcraft, female dogs, and most importantly, crossroads. Hecate had a connection to basically every goddess of femininity and fate, as well as any who represented hidden mysteries. Her three faces are, once again, the maiden, the wife or mother, and the crone. These three stages of a woman's life are the three deaths for Plath in "Lady Lazarus": maiden at ten, wife as a young woman, and then crone at the ripe old age of thirty. The loss of virginity is the death of innocence required to become a wife or a mother. When one has finished having her babies, and possibly lost her marriage, it is another kind of death. Hecate is often depicted bearing torches like a particular female statue we will soon look at in this book.

Brigit (or Brigid, or Brig) is the Irish pagan goddess equivalent to Isis and Venus. Her name means "exalted one," and she is the goddess of the dawn. In pre-Christian times, women tended a flame in her honor. In Lady Gregory's famous retelling of Irish myths, poets worshipped her. Plath certainly also knew Brigit from Joseph Campbell:

> "from a fire below comes the voice of the virgin lady of the isle – the goddess Brigit, who became St. Bridget when baptized. 'Mishe mishe,' she says in her native tongue, "I am, I am…"

People who know Plath's poetry and fiction have seen that "I am, I am" before across her work. Brigit/Bridget represents Mother Ireland to James Joyce in *Finnegans Wake*.

The ancient Greek goddess Hera was the queen of the Olympian gods. She was said to be married to Zeus, who cheated on her relentlessly. Maybe Plath related? Hera was jealous and had such a temper that even Zeus feared her retribution for his illegitimate children and adulteries. She was the protector of women and heroes.

Meet Bast/Frige

> "She had wrapped her marble-like body in a huge fur, and rolled herself up trembling like a cat."
> —Leopold von Sacher-Masoch, *Venus in Furs*

We saw cats and the lioness in the last mirror of Alchemy. As you read on, you will start to notice often how one mirror overlaps into others, reinforcing the strength of Plath's poem as a whole. By now you're getting it.

The Egyptian cat goddess, Eye of Ra, had the body of a woman and the head of a lioness. Cats are connected to Bastet, an Egyptian solar deity, and instrument of the sun god's vengeance. Centuries later, Bastet's head evolved into that of a domestic cat's and, like Isis/Venus, she became associated with motherhood and fertility.

Norse myth, from Plath's heritage, holds that there were nine worlds in the same way that a cat has nine lives, and these worlds also appear to correspond with the first nine stations of the Qabalah. Welsh legend tells of the Cath Palug, a massive predatory cat that killed and ate "nine score warriors," again like Plath's nine lives in the seventh stanza.

The day of Friday is named after Frige, Norse goddess of romantic love, for her association with the planet Venus. Her chariot is said to be drawn by cats, and Frige is sometimes equated with Freya, another love goddess. Both goddesses were said to have married Odin and to have shamanistic skills and perform rituals of symbolic death, dismemberment, and resurrection.

Meet G-1 and Lady Shark Fin

Here's where it gets really weird: Quetzalcoatl (pronounced *ket-sahl-koh-aht-l*), central Mexico's equivalent to the goddess Venus we've been reading about, is identified with the goddess G-1.

That's the letter G and the number one, according to a coded system used to translate this language that no one speaks any longer. The goddess G-1 is a sea deity sometimes understood to have characteristics of a shark. The shark will have significance when we get to the "History and the World" mirror. In the meantime, G-1's Mayan calendar birthday is "9 Ik with 9 Wind."

Nines again. More echoing of Plath's nine lives. And a shark on The Lovers card? Not as ridiculous as you might think. Get a load of that giant triangular dark dorsal fin of a mountain between Adam and Eve. Or Lilith, as it were. This mountain, called the Mountain of Initiation or the Mystic Mountain of Abiegnus, is the port of entry to visit Venus the goddess. Yeats wrote that this mountain protects "the great walled garden of Eden."

We know for sure that Plath knew all about the ancient Mexicans and especially the Aztec/Mayan[16] god Quetzalcoatl from one of her favorite books, *The Golden Bough*. She also sent a picture postcard in 1955 from the British Museum featuring a page from the Codex Zouche-Nuttal, a Pre-Columbian Mixtec pictographic manuscript from Mexico. She may however have been introduced to Aztec gods first, most surprisingly, from *The Story of the Book of Mormon*, which she read in high school working on a 25-page thesis on Mormonism. Plath took an interest in history and mythology of all kinds, and she began to appreciate Mexican art.

In 1959, Plath and Hughes hung around a bit with author Selden Rodman[17], an American art critic, and historian of Latin American and Caribbean history, who may have introduced her to the subject. In her journal, she implied that she had read at least one of Rodman's books and wrote about seeing murals by the Mexican artist José Clemente Orozco:

> To art: Orozco: the murals at Dartmouth the history of the Indians. A Christ-the-tiger hacking down his own cross & the statues of classicism, Buddhism. The great white god Quetzalcoatl banishing the false crew of gods of death, magic, fire, storms.

Even more impressive than the plumed serpent Quetzalcoatl is the real-life Mayan goddess, the celebrated 8th-century Yaxchilán queen Ix Kábal Xook (or Xoc), also known as Lady Shark Fin. From the lintel carvings in her temple, built by her king in 726 C.E., anthropologists know that she was the most powerful woman in early Mesoamerica. In these drawings, she is depicted summoning a deity, performing sacrificial rituals, and doing other actions no

---

[16] The Mayans called this same feathered serpent god *Kukulkan*.
[17] Cary Selden Rodman (1909-2002) was a prolific US writer of poetry, plays, prose, political commentary, Latin American and Caribbean history, biography and travel writing. Plath considered Rodman to have written *the* authoritative book on Haiti at that time.

female of that civilization had ever done before or since. Lady Shark Fin was one of a kind.

It was believed that the movement of the planets, Moon, and Sun synchronized with the Yaxchilán kings and Lady Shark Fin. Structure 23, the Queen's Quarters for Lady Shark Fin, is called "bee's house" (another Plathian image for her later bee poems) and this house is where the queen's bones reside. Plath must have loved the correspondences to her own life, and who she would have liked to be. Lady Shark Fin's name has been engraved on her bones, which also sounds a little bit like sorting the body pieces in Plath's "These are my hands / My knees."

There are numerous images of shark-like creatures in Aztec and Mayan art. Although much of these civilizations lived in the forest, dangerous man-eating bull sharks have been known to come up the rivers into the mainland. Coastal natives hunted sharks and traveled into the interior carrying their teeth and jaws, which were often used for jewelry, weapons, and blood-letting. Shark fin designs adorn Central American Indian pottery and are found on the walls of ceremonial buildings as well.

Whether called Eve or Lilith, Aphrodite or Venus, man has driven the show, and women are said to have dual natures: either goodness (virginity and motherhood) or evil (temptresses and destroyers). What it comes down to is this: No matter what we call her—Eve, Lilith, Lucifer, The White Goddess, The Triple Goddess, Aphrodite, Bast, Frige, Cat, Shark, Venus, or Isis—we are talking about the same powerful symbol of femininity with the ability to create, to destroy men, and resurrect. Oh, and you best treat her as an equal or she'll eat you up!

CHAPTER SEVEN

Fourth Mirror: History and World Events

Plath's Evocation of History in "Lady Lazarus"

Excerpt from a 1962 interview with Sylvia Plath by Peter Orr:

PLATH: "Well now, you are talking to me as a general American. In particular, my background is, may I say, German and Austrian. On one side I am a first-generation American, on one side I'm second-generation American, and so my concern with concentration camps and so on is uniquely intense. And then, again, I'm rather a political person as well, so I suppose that's what part of it comes from."

ORR: "And as a poet, do you have a great and keen sense of the historic?"

PLATH: "I am not a historian, but I find myself being more and more fascinated by history and now I find myself reading more and more about history. I am very interested in Napoleon, at the present: I'm very interested in battles, in wars, in Gallipoli, the First World War and so on, and I think that as I age I am becoming more and more historical. I certainly wasn't at all in my early twenties."

It really is amazing how much Plath came right out and told us about her methods and thinking. Still, we don't seem to see Plath telling us our own history. We keep looking to Plath's work only for *her* personal stories. There's no denying the presence of Germany and World War II in "Lady Lazarus." Plath shines a searchlight on Nazi images beginning in the second stanza, followed by some choice symbols of the Holocaust and the German honorific for a man, *Herr*. Incredibly, Hitler's Nazi party, in an attempt to return to what they believed to be their cultural history, based their idealism in part in German neopaganism and Norse mythology, which Plath touched upon in the last mirrors with a nod to the goddess Frige. Rooted in mysticism and the occult, neopaganism ascribes "a charge" to even inanimate objects. A *charge* is their term for a soul, corresponding with Plath's nineteenth stanza. German neopagans believed (and some still do) in fate and destiny, attributes of The Lovers tarot card. From her beloved book, *The Golden Bough*, Plath knew about neopaganism, its history and practices, and that women were worshiped by ancient Germans.

German neopaganism incorporated practices such as runes, astrology, ritual magic, and the idea of a pure Aryan blood line, reworking Nordic magical tradition to better serve the state. The Thule Society was created to preserve the secrets of German antiquity, and members believed that Hitler was the redeemer of the motherland. Prominent members of the Nazi party were a part of this society which proposed that the ancient wheel of life, the swastika, be used to represent the Nazis. Heinrich Himmler, the leader of the SS, had a great interest in mysticism and emulated the structure of St. Ignatius Loyola's Jesuit order. We know that Ted Hughes read *The Spiritual Exercises of St. Ignatius* during his time with Plath.

You saw in the first mirror that the number ten is a milestone number and has much mystical significance. One school of thought says that the strongest earthquakes, volcanic eruptions, storms and tsunamis, droughts and pandemics seem to take place about every ten years, reflecting Plath's first stanza. Once every ten years is also the frequency of the population census for the United States and the United Kingdom, a "walking" count of citizens that first began around the time of the Black Death. Plath had a book about the United States Census in her personal library, so she knew all about this too.

The Passion Play

> "I started writing this play twelve years ago after re-reading a childhood book which includes an account of Oberammergau in the early 1900s. In this old-fashioned narrative, the man who played Christ was actually so holy as to have become His living embodiment. The woman who played Mary was, in real life, just as pure as the Virgin. I started thinking, how would it shape or misshape a life to play a biblical role year after year? How are we scripted? Where is the line between authentic identity and performance? And is there, in fact, such a line?"
> —Playwright Sarah Ruhl, notes on *Passion Play*

More significantly relevant to "Lady Lazarus" is that once every decade the famous Passion Play is performed in Oberammergau, Germany. This play was important to Plath, because her high-school class took a trip to Europe to attend it. Plath did not have the money to join them.

The Passion Play began during the Thirty Years' War, the age Plath gives in the seventh stanza of "Lady Lazarus." It was the 17th century when the village of Oberammergau swore to God to perform "The Play of Suffering, Death, and Resurrection of our Lord Jesus Christ," to hold back the Black Death that had decimated its people. During this time, Jews were blamed for poisoning wells and were sometimes burned alive. More than two hundred Jewish communities were attacked across Europe, and more than three hundred and fifty massacres took place.

Cats too were considered as allies of the devil and of witches at this time, so the people killed them in great numbers (this was a big mistake, because cats ate mice and rats, which we found out later were the carriers of the plague). Plath's details of the corpse and death shroud, of dying, and the burning of bodies to prevent contamination are woven throughout "Lady Lazarus." With almost half the population of Europe killed from the plague, it took "A miracle!" to knock it out.

Jumping ahead to the 20th century, Adolf Hitler and the Nazi party were extremely taken with the Passion Play. Exploiting the 1934 jubilee season, the Ministry of Public Enlightenment and Propaganda pushed its anti-Semitic themes and encouraged the public to see it. Their posters read, "Germany is calling you!" fitting the call of Plath's fourteenth stanza. In her interview with Peter Orr, Plath continued:

> "...one should be able to manipulate these experiences with an informed and an intelligent mind. I think that personal experience is very important, but certainly it shouldn't be a kind of shut-box and mirror-looking, narcissistic experience. I believe it should be *relevant,* and relevant to the larger things, the bigger things such as Hiroshima and Dachau and so on."

Ah, I promised you History ...and the World. Well, here is the World part:

Just When You Thought it was Safe to Go Back in the Water

> "Sharks have everything a scientist dreams of. They're beautiful—God, how beautiful they are! They're like an impossibly perfect piece of machinery. They're as graceful as any bird. They're as mysterious as any animal on earth. No one knows

for sure how long they live or what impulses—except for hunger—they respond to. There are more than two hundred and fifty species of shark, and everyone is different from every other one."
—Peter Benchley, author of *Jaws*

While the novel *Jaws* was written after Plath's time, we do know that she read a lot about plants and animals, and imagery from these sources often crept into her work. Take, for example, the dark triangular mountain pictured in the background between the couple on The Lovers tarot card. We first mentioned this in the Mythology mirror, and it calls to mind the Mayan shark goddess G-1 because it isn't a stretch to say that image of a mountain closely resembles a shark fin. And the real-life goddess, Lady Shark Fin, of course.

Much of "Lady Lazarus" fits the predatory tiger shark with its cat-like name, and the Great White shark, both known to be man-eaters, as in Plath's last line. Why wouldn't the perfect killing machine consider dying an "art"? From its "featureless" face, a prominent nose, blank eye "pits," and a "full set of teeth," the shark is well-described in "Lady Lazarus." The largest sharks are female and always "smiling." The shark might certainly ask, "O my enemy. / Do I terrify?" Great White sharks are known to live thirty years and longer, fitting Plath's seventh stanza line, "I am only thirty." Sharks are known to eat a lot of trash, often revealed when the belly is slit in front of crowds of people who shove in to look at the beast hung from its tail. It was not unusual to witness "a million" camera flashes on these occasions. Nine species of shark inhabit Atlantic waters, like Plath's cat's nine lives.

Cousin of the tiger shark, the Lazarus shark of the Great Barrier Reef walks on its fins along the coral—a fit for Plath's miraculous walking in the second stanza. When the tide washes out, the fish is often stranded on dry land. Yet it survives for hours without oxygen in a coma-like state. Like Lazarus's resurrection, this shark returns to life when the tide washes it back to sea. Lazarus sharks eat worms and mollusks—Plath's fourteenth stanza. Also fitting the

"Lady Lazarus" poem is the Lucifer shark or Blackbelly lanternshark. With its luminescent belly, the Lucifer shark is lit like the Nazi lampshade of the second stanza. All sharks have keen electroceptor sensing organs ("a million filaments") to detect the charge of electric fields in water, corresponding to Lucifer's/Venus's light and Plath's nineteenth stanza "charge."

The Venus Flytrap

> "The Venus flytrap, a devouring organism, aptly named for the goddess of love."
> —Tennessee Williams, from *Suddenly Last Summer*

Here's another wonderful reflection within this mirror: Called "the most wonderful plants in the world" by Charles Darwin, the carnivorous Venus flytrap shares the name Venus, along with shark-like characteristics including those smiling teeth known as cilia, which close around insect prey. With its Luciferian correspondence, the plant tolerates fire well and needs regular burnings of its land to keep competition from taking it over. And, get this: the Venus flytrap may live to be up to thirty years old. Plath knew all about this from her College Botany book.

Okay. Now let's get back to History, because we've got the story of stories here, and all of it is true:

The Statue of Liberty

> "The Statue of Liberty is no longer saying, 'Give me your poor, your tired, your huddled masses.' She's got a baseball bat and yelling, 'You want a piece of me?'"
> —Robin Williams

When America was asked to foot the bill for the Statue of Liberty's pedestal in an economic depression, *The New York Times* wrote, "no true patriot can countenance any such expenditures for bronze females in the present state of our finances." Can you believe that? Just a few generations ago society could so openly declare that women weren't worth the effort and expense.

Despite the fight, she *was* built! And yet, when the Statue of Liberty was complete, outside of the designers' wives, women were not even allowed to attend the public ceremony. Suffragists, the women protesting and fighting for equality, appreciated the big ironic joke of forbidding women to witness the unveiling of a female statue. "American women have no liberty," read a protester's sign on a barge in the Hudson River before thousands of spectators the day that Lady Liberty made her debut, October 28, 1886. The Votes-for-Women protesters circled Bedloe's Island in their boat and took this momentous opportunity to make speeches about equality by megaphone from the water. "If Liberty got down off her pedestal, she would not have been allowed to vote in either France or America," they said.

Hey, I know the world can seem like it's a pretty bad place today, but be glad you didn't live as a woman just a mere hundred years ago.

Margaret Fuller and Feminism

"I am 'too fiery' ... yet I wish to be seen as I am, and would lose all rather than soften away anything."—Margaret Fuller

Sylvia Plath read a *lot*. We know this for sure, and there are innumerable references to whatever was her latest page-turner that day in her journals, letters, and notebooks. In addition to novels and poetry, she read many biographies and history books. Her mother Aurelia said that the book *A Short History of Women* by Langdon-Davies was well marked and "held particular significance for her." Through those formative years, Plath surrounded herself with strong female mentors, such as professor Mary Ellen Chase at Smith College, and Dr. Dorothea Krook at Cambridge. When Plath wrote "Lady Lazarus," there seemed to be a critical mass of these strong women finding their feminist power. Plath herself seemed to think her power started brewing a little bit earlier. In April 1956, she wrote: "I am growing and shall be a woman beyond women for my strength." This might not be how things actually worked out for her, but that was the intention.

In May of that year, Plath published an article in Oxford University's *Isis* magazine, calling for "a new culture at Cambridge in which a female student "keeps her female status while being accepted as a human being." Still, she wrestled back and forth with the social pressure of choosing marriage and motherhood over a career. In her novel *The Bell Jar*, Plath's character Esther believed that to choose a career over marriage was to deny her femininity. She wanted to be sexy and beautiful, no doubt. Yet, in her journals, Plath wrote:

> "to realize that most American males worship woman as a sex machine with rounded breasts and a convenient opening in the vagina, as a painted doll who shouldn't have a thought in her pretty head other than cooking a steak dinner and comforting him in bed after a hard 9-5 day at a routine business job. * to realize that there are some men who like a girl as a companion in mind as well as body…"

and

> "I think that is why there are so many women's clubs and organizations. They've got to feel emancipated and self important somehow. God Forbid that I become a Crusader. But I might surprise myself, and become a second Lucretia Mott[18] or something equivalent.

As a history buff, Plath also knew quite a lot about the writers, reformers and activists from Massachusetts. Despite the social molding that contributed to her confusion, Plath grew up with feminist author heroes such as Louisa May Alcott. In her journals

---

[18] Lucretia Mott (1793-1880), abolitionist, women's rights activist and social reformer. Also from Massachusetts, Mott was a Quaker pacifist influenced by Unitarians. Mott has been called "the greatest American woman of the nineteenth century."

she wrote of having had dinner at the home of the grand-daughter of Julia Ward Howe. The movers and shakers in women's suffrage and anti-slavery seemed to all be Massachusetts women, and American journalist, author, poet, literary critic and Unitarian transcendentalist, Margaret Fuller (1810-1850) led the pack.

Plath shared much in common with Fuller, given a background in Transcendentalism from a Unitarian background. Fuller was born in Cambridge, Massachusetts, Plath's home state, and there were numerous biographies written about Fuller in Plath's time, including one by Julia Ward Howe. Fuller wrote what is considered to be the first feminist work, *Woman in the Nineteenth Century*. Originally entitled *The Great Lawsuit: Man versus Men, Woman versus Women*, this 1845 work made Fuller one of the most important figures in the women's rights movement, and her rebelliousness and independence inspired the Nathaniel Hawthorne character Hester Prynne in *The Scarlet Letter*. Fuller was hired as the first female editor of Ralph Waldo Emerson's *The Dial* and became good friends with Emerson, as would the poet Emma Lazarus (yes, Lazarus; no coincidence there), who is seen in the Arts and Humanities mirror of this poem. Fuller, Lazarus, and Plath all shared an obsession with their fathers. Fuller wrote, "My father's image follows me constantly." Fuller died in a shipwreck off Fire Island, fire being another shared image in the "Lady Lazarus" poem. Even more fascinating, Fuller had written about an omen of her early death.

Sojourner Truth

"...I pay the penalty of the educated, emancipated woman"
—Sylvia Plath

If there's one thing we know, it's that if the name of a black woman born into slavery in the year 1797 is still mentioned today, she did something extraordinary. Of course, for so many African-

Americans at this time, survival alone counted as extraordinary. But Sojourner Truth did much more.

In the year 1883, the same year that Lazarus wrote "The New Colossus," African-American activist Sojourner Truth died. Truth's history had been a hard one. She was born into slavery and taken from her mother and sold at the age of nine. *Nine.* That is not only ridiculously painful to contemplate, but it also reflects on Plath's "nine lives" in the poem.

As an adult, Truth fled to Northampton, Massachusetts, home of Plath's Smith College, to live in a mixed-race utopian community that supported abolition and suffrage. Truth gave a famous speech later stylized as "Ain't I a Woman?", referencing the Bible story of Lazarus and the importance of his sisters Mary and Martha in their appeal to Jesus to raise their brother, as a case for women's rights. Let's stop for a second and take this all in: Emma Lazarus. Sojourner Truth. Women's Rights and Northampton, Massachusetts. You see how it all circles back to Plath's world.

Despite never learning to read or write, Truth delivered one of the most captivating and emotionally powerful speeches in women's rights history at the Women's Convention in Akron, Ohio on May 29, 1851. It is her most famous. According to the first published version of that speech, Truth said:

> "I want to say a few words about this matter. I am a woman's rights. [*sic*] I have as much muscle as any man, and can do as much work as any man. I have plowed and reaped and husked and chopped and mowed, and can any man do more than that? I have heard much about the sexes being equal. I can carry as much as any man, and can eat as much too, if I can get it. I am as strong as any man that is now. As for intellect, all I can say is, if a woman have a pint, and a man a quart—why can't she have her little pint full? You need not be afraid to give us our rights for fear we will take too much, —for we can't take more than our pint'll hold. The poor men seems to be all in confusion, and don't know what to do. Why children, if you have woman's rights, give it to her and you will feel better. You will have your own rights, and they won't be so much trouble. I can't read, but I can hear. I have heard the bible and have learned that Eve caused man to sin.

> Well, if woman upset the world, do give her a chance to set it right side up again. The Lady has spoken about Jesus, how he never spurned woman from him, and she was right. When Lazarus died, Mary and Martha came to him with faith and love and besought him to raise their brother. And Jesus wept and Lazarus came forth. And how came Jesus into the world? Through God who created him and the woman who bore him. Man, where was your part? But the women are coming up blessed be God and a few of the men are coming up with them. But man is in a tight place, the poor slave is on him, woman is coming on him, he is surely between a hawk and a buzzard."[19]

Was it Truth's determination to advance women and people of color that spoke to Plath? Or was it her ability to survive and rise from the ash? Plath knew that since ancient Greece, women were disregarded and made to be slaves. Truth's speech, later revised by abolitionists and retitled "Ain't I a Woman?" along with Plath's "Lady Lazarus," both ask bold, unanswered questions, and deliver answers to the questions society was afraid to ask. Both the speech and poem reflect The Lovers tarot card as "one who passes through all manner of tests and trials, both of his physical and mental strength."

In the more popular version of this speech, recorded by Frances Gage (because Truth could not read or write), ends with a reference to Lilith:

> "If the first woman God ever made was strong enough to turn the world upside down all alone, these women together ought to be able to turn it back, and get it right side up again! And now they are asking to do it, the men better let them."

Truth spoke as a woman first, and then as a person of color. Truth did not end her speech threatening to "eat men like air," as does Plath in her poem. But she came close.

---

[19] There is a famous version of this speech written in imitation of a Southern Negro slave's dialect, but historians have proven Truth never lived in the South and this is incorrect. Nevertheless, there is a great reading of it online by author Alice Walker at http://sojournertruthmemorial.org/sojourner-truth/her-words/.

The Japanese Woman

起死回生

"Wake from death and return to life."
—*Japanese idiom, meaning to turn a bad or desperate situation into a success*

Meanwhile, on the other side of the world, Plath was aware that women in Japan had a parallel fight for their rights. Before her death, Plath made a recording of "Lady Lazarus" with additional lines that her editor friend Al Alvarez encouraged her to cut. One of those lines referenced being Japanese. You can still hear this and other deleted parts in Plath's recorded reading of this poem, which is easily found online. [20]

Plath read Japanese imagist poetry, and knew about Japanese culture and Geisha girls in her news magazines, and she was especially interested in Japanese arts of all kinds. In her journals, she longs for American films to be of the quality of the Japanese, Swedish and Italians. Plath also compares scenery to Japanese watercolors, and wrote of her impression of Japanese dancers at an arts festival:

> "Gagaku Japanese Dancers. Weird, odd, but I went into a trance. The high pipey, drumskin music, jars of water, blown reeds. The raised royal stage. Red cinnabar, gold. And the stepping and bowing, the delicate stylized patterns of four and two. Orange sleeves, planes of embroidered color. Headdresses of gold and silver. The animal-faced prince. The lovely dance before the cave of the sun-goddess, with a bough of green to which was attached a white circlet, shaping the air, now against the green, now hanging from it, a supplication. Then the sabers, the spears. A cold, wet night, the soil squishy underfoot, people with woolen rugs, hats, scarves, layers of sweaters. A few drops of chill rain. Low dark skies. Winds of merciless damp."

---

[20] Due to copyright restrictions, I am not able to share the excised line with you here.

A suffrage movement in Japan occurred at the same time as in the United States, and with forced prostitution and polygamy, Japanese women had even harder lives than women in the U.S. and Britain. By seeing herself as "identical" in her womanhood, Plath wrote in kinship with these women who had become America's enemies in World War II. It seems that Plath examined women's rights all over the world, throughout the ages. Even women in the seemingly enlightened society of ancient Greece, the era from which Lady Liberty is modeled, had no citizenship and no right to vote. Female repression and feminist uprising had become a worldwide, timeless shared experience.

Frege's Puzzle for Equality

> "Equality gives rise to challenging questions which are not altogether easy to answer. [...] The discovery that the rising sun is not new every morning, but always the same, was one of the most fertile astronomical discoveries. Even today the identification of a small planet or a comet is not always a matter of course. Now if we were to regard equality as a relation between that which the names 'a' and 'b' designate, it would seem that $a = b$ could not differ from $a = a$ (i.e. provided $a = b$ is true). A relation would thereby be expressed of a thing to itself, and indeed one in which each thing stands to itself but to no other thing."
> —Gottlob Frege, "On Sense and Reference," 1892

Interweaving Greek mythology, astronomy and the world, the ancient Greeks named the evening star, or Venus, "Hesperus." Hesperus was believed to be the son of the dawn goddess, Eos. The short phrase, "Hesperus is Phosphorus" is known as Frege's Puzzle (a homophone to the Nordic goddess "Frige"). A famous philosophy of language, its principle is that if one knows the meanings of these words, he cannot rationally accept that one is more powerful than the other. It is a semantic statement about equality.

One of Frege's best and most famous students was the German Jewish professor Gershom Scholem, considered to be the founder of modern Kabbalah studies and the first professor of Jewish mysticism at the Hebrew University of Jerusalem. Ironically, Frege was a Nazi sympathizer who tended to make exceptions.[21] It is probably no accident Plath used "So, so" in her twenty-third stanza, as "so-and-so" is originally a Jewish expression.[22] And as an interesting aside, "Soso" was also Soviet dictator Joseph Stalin's nickname.

Frankism and its Holy Mistress

> "We are given to the cult of personality; when things go badly we look to some messiah to save us. If by chance we think we have found one, it will not be long before we destroy him."
> –Constantine Karamanlis

The title "Herr Doktor" was a common address for the German-born Gershom Scholem, who fled to Palestine during wartime. In addition to being the great scholar of Kabbalah, Scholem is known for his writings on Jacob Frank and Frankism—yet another perfect historical fit for "Lady Lazarus." Scholem called Frank "a degenerate," but was still fascinated enough to study him. See, the Jewish religion, like so many others, has had its share of division and sects. The biggies were the Sabbateans and the Hasidic movements, and Frankism came out of Sabbateanism, when Jacob Frank claimed that he was the reincarnation of the Sabbatean messiah.

Born in 1726, Jacob Frank was a Jew who rejected the Torah and converted to both Islam and Catholicism. While the Christians were busy with the Crusades and executing Jews by the thousands, Frank led a mass conversion where hundreds of followers publicly renounced Judaism to avoid being put to death. At the height of his popularity, up to 30,000 (ex-)Jews followed him.

---

[21] Frege shows up again in the *Fixed Stars Govern a Life* interpretation of Plath's "The Detective."
[22] *Decoding Sylvia Plath's Bee Poems* will have an interpretation of "Wintering" with more on "so-and-so."

This all relates to "Lady Lazarus," I promise.

Frank created Frankism, a mystical religion in 18th-century Poland, combining elements of Christianity and Judaism. Known for Rasputin-like behaviors of both asceticism and sensuality, Frankists practiced orgies and sexual rites, as well as self-flagellation as religious penance.[23] Frankists ignored all prohibitions and restrictions of Jewish law, including incest, and they rejected the Talmud, recognizing only the Kabbalah and Zohar as sacred texts. The rabbinical court accused Frank of breaking fundamental Jewish laws of morality and modesty, much as the Pharisees condemned Jesus for raising Lazarus. Back in 1756, these rabbis demanded that the Frankists be burned at the stake as heretics, and most of the society agreed.

Frank's daughter, Eva Frank, was the only woman to have been declared a Jewish messiah, as well as the incarnation of the female aspect of God, *Shekhinah*, and the reincarnation of the Virgin Mary. In the Kabbalah's sacred text, *The Zohar*, Shekhinah is "a beautiful maiden who has no eyes," reminiscent of the fifth stanza of the poem "Lady Lazarus" (Don't forget, it all comes back to the poem!). Upon Jacob Frank's death in 1791, Eva became the Frankist "holy mistress" and leader of the cult. It all fits with the more sexual themes of The Lovers card, and their history seems to run all through "Lady Lazarus" as well.

Astoundingly, some of Frank's followers went on to become prominent political and social leaders in Prague and elsewhere, and Adam Mickiewicz, considered to be Poland's greatest poet, espoused and used Frankist themes in his writing. Frankists tend to support the Frankfort School (cultural Marxism); large-scale, non-selective immigration; Deconstructivism/Critical Theory; corporate leftism; sexual liberty; and radical jurisprudence. Conspiracy theories abound that Frankists evolved into Freemasons, and many people of power and wealth in America, including three Supreme

---

[23] See *Fixed Stars Govern a Life's* interpretation of Plath's poem "Tulips" for more on Rasputin.

Court Justices.[24] Sabbatean-Frankists, mostly German Jews, have been linked to a few regions, such as Prague, Frankfurt, and Posen, the latter being Otto Plath's hometown. Kabbalist Gershom Scholem is said to have claimed, "Frank will always be remembered as one of the most frightening phenomena in the whole of Jewish history. Psychologist Sigmund Freud, Communist leader Karl Marx, and Emma Lazarus are all considered to be "neo-Frankists" by conspiracy theorists.

Let's backtrack for a second, and recap some key themes of "Lady Lazarus": You identified where we see aspects of The Lovers card's symbols, sensuality, and the fight for equality in this poem. You picked up on the alchemical elements, with all that copper and fire and burning. You certainly understand the feminine oppression and a fight for freedom in the historical aspects. You put it together that femininity is represented by the goddess Venus who goes by many other names, including Isis, Lucifer, Aphrodite, and Frige. You've learned about and maybe even noted to read up on some major female historical powerhouses, such as Lady Shark Fin, Sojourner Truth, Margaret Fuller, and Emma Lazarus. And you've seen a couple of surprising ways men like Frege and Frank handled equality in the past. Now, watch how Plath finishes this amazing balancing act in the next two mirrors!

---

[24] Supreme Court Justice Cardozo, who is cousin to Emma Lazarus, Frankfurter, and Brandeis are all said to come from Sabbatean or Frankist dynasties. True? I dunno.

CHAPTER EIGHT

Fifth Mirror: Astrology and Astronomy

Orbiting Venus

"It is ridiculous for us to separate our forces when it is such a magnificently 'aspected' year…"
—Sylvia Plath talking astrology in a letter to her mother, October 28, 1956

As mentioned earlier, we tend to equate the angel Lucifer, clearly named in "Lady Lazarus," with the devil. However, you also learned a couple chapters back that Lucifer is known as the goddess Venus or Isis as well. The brightest visible body in the night sky, Venus is called both the morning and the evening star, and Isis, as a goddess and *not* the Islamic State terror faction, embodies feminine power.

Most interesting is the fact that the planet Venus, named after the goddess, for centuries has been the only planet in the solar system named after any female. Venus rotates on its axis clockwise, the opposite direction from the other planets. We know that Plath could identify Venus, because she wrote in her pocket calendar notes on May 26, 1956, "Venus in clear bluegreen sky." When Plath wrote "Lady Lazarus" in October 1962, the American spacecraft Mariner 2 was in Venus's orbit. Almost as a metaphor for women's rights, Mariner 2 faced continuous setbacks. It lost power and overheated, yet it persevered on its emigration from Earth to this new world.

> "And if there are swamps, why not cyacads and dragonflies and perhaps even dinosaurs on Venus? Observation: there was absolutely nothing to see on Venus. Conclusion: It must be covered with life. The featureless clouds of Venus reflected our own predispositions. We are alive, and we resonate with the idea of life elsewhere. But only careful accumulation and assessment of the evidence can tell us whether a given world is inhabited. Venus turns out not to oblige our predispositions.
> —Carl Sagan, *Cosmos*

As you can see from these words by our friend Carl Sagan, the planet Venus was considered to be a disc without features, hidden under a veil of linen-like clouds, corresponding to Plath's third and fourth stanzas. Yet the Mariner 2 spacecraft revealed a pitted surface, like Plath's image of eyepits, and the most active volcanoes of any planet known at the time. Venus is believed to periodically undergo entire planetary resurfacing; one might compare that to resurrection. Its "flesh" is self-consumed; the grave is her home surface. Nothing can live on Venus, corresponding well with Plath's death-and-dying theme.

Brighter than any star and seen even in the daytime, Venus is the "Evening Star" that becomes the "Morning Star" as it overtakes the Earth in its orbit of the Sun. Plath knew from *The Unicorn* that Yeats called it this, and that he even attempted to commune with planetary spirits of Venus. Despite the time of day or night, she is the "same, identical" planet. Like Isis is Frige is Venus is Aphrodite. Like *Hesperus is Phosphorus*. Like women around the world who have gone through the same stuff.

Plath's filament image is not limited to describing the tungsten filament inside of a light bulb; a solar filament is a prominence extending from the Sun, viewed as something dark against its bright background. This is true when Venus transits the sun, an astrologically important time for women on Earth.[25] Venus has a slow rotation, paralleling Plath's poetic turning and burning. One Venus day is equivalent to about ten Earth days, which has another reflection in "Lady Lazarus." A mystery of Venus is its "ashen light" on its dark side, Plath's ash image. The Mayan calendar is based, in part, on the motion of Venus. The calendar ends in 2012, and considering the gender given to her, at the end of the Mayan world, she fits with Plath's last line, "And I eat men like air."

The Maternalistic Pawnee

> "All things in the world are two. In our minds we are two, good and evil. With our eyes we see two things, things that are fair and things that are ugly. . .We have the right hand that strikes and makes for evil, and we have the left hand full of kindness, near the heart. One foot may lead us to an evil way, the other foot may lead us to a good. So are all things two, all two."
> —Eagle Chief (Letakos-Lesa), Pawnee

This quotation especially fits The Lovers tarot card, as well as Plath's obsession with her own dual nature. Crossing both Astronomy and World mirrors are the Pawnee Indians of North America, devout cosmologists, who believed that the Morning Star and Evening Star (the planet Venus) mated to create the first human, bringing us back around to that creation story on The Lovers tarot card once again. This is all told in one of Plath's favorite books, *The Golden Bough*, and in *Finnegans Wake*, Joyce

---

[25] Historical events coinciding with the Venus transit are throughout *Fixed Stars Govern a Life*'s interpretation of Plath's poem, "A Secret."

calls it the "Radium Wedding of Night and Morning." But back to the Pawnee: the Pawnee believed that the first human was a girl. The Pawnee were very female-centered, and designed their lodges to correspond to the universe and the womb. A young girl was ritually sacrificed to the Morning Star each spring, and one might see this myth woven into "Lady Lazarus," too—especially because Plath's husband Ted Hughes studied anthropology, read extensively about Native American cultures, and believed "the Red Indians" to be "the last sane human beings."[26]

Mayan Astronomy

The ancient Mayans tracked the heavens long before Copernicus and viewed the stars and planets from the Caracol observatory at Chichen Itza in Mexico. We know they watched there the regular path of Venus through the year with a particular interest. They associated Venus with war, and so major battles were scheduled to coincide with her celestial moments. The famous Dresden codex, a key to reading Mayan symbols and the oldest surviving book in the Americas, contains a Venus almanac as well as other astronomical observations. Anthropologists know absolutely that the Mayan people watched and recorded the pattern of comets too. In the Mythology mirror of "Lady Lazarus," Lady Shark Fin was a major player in coordinating her civilization's actions with astronomy.

Halley's Comet

> "Aristotle's opinion…that comets were nothing else than sublunary vapors or airy meteors…prevailed so far amongst the Greeks, that this sublimest part of astronomy lay altogether neglected; since none could think it worthwhile to observe, and to give an account of the wandering and uncertain paths of vapours floating in the Ether."
> —Edmond Halley, astronomer

---

[26] Hughes wrote this in a letter to his brother Gerald dated 25 November 1974.

Comets are mythologically associated with women and girls, going back to a story of the two daughters of Orion blessed by the goddesses Athene and Aphrodite. They sacrificed themselves to end a plague, and in return, the goddesses turned them into comets. An earlier draft of Plath's "Lady Lazarus" mentions two daughters.

There is another comet-related myth in which Electra, one of the Pleiades, tore out her hair in a fit of rage and it became a comet.

The word comet originates from the Greek *komē*, meaning "the hair on one's head." Plath's rising and red hair in "Lady Lazarus" fit well.

We know that Halley's Comet (actually pronounced "Hawley's" but almost everybody says it wrong), which comes by once about every seventy-five years, has been observed and recorded since Babylonian times. It's also known as "1P" because it was the first periodic comet identified. Much as the planet Venus rotates in its own direction, Halley's Comet is described as "retrograde," meaning that it travels in the direction opposite that of planetary orbits.

Ancient astronomers considered comets to be an enormous fire in the sky. Comets were blamed for tsunamis, earthquakes, and plagues. From the Roman Empire on, comets became connected with human-related disasters: death, riots, war and slaughter. Julius Caesar was said to have died during a comet's transit, and his son Augustus claimed that his father rode it onward to heaven.

In 218 C.E., a Roman historian labeled Halley's Comet "a very fearful star." In 451 Halley's Comet appeared before the defeat of Attila the Hun and began to gain its notoriety for the downfall of empires. In 684 we see the first known Japanese records of the comet, while on the western side of the world, there was a three-month rainstorm and outbreak of Black Death during the event.

In 837 Halley's Comet was described as appearing as bright as Venus. Halley's Comet showed up on a medieval tapestry in 1066, and was called "a hairy star" and "a portent." During Halley's Comet in 1145, Harold II, the King of England, fought William I, the Duke of Normandy. William won the Battle of Hastings and succeeded to the English throne. It's no wonder then that Halley's Comet continued to be read as "the death of an emperor." In 1222 Japanese astronomers noted the comet was "as large as the half Moon…its color was white but its rays were red." Artist Giotto di Bondone included the comet in his painting "The Adoration of the Magi" in the year 1301.

Around the same time that opponents of slavery came to reject colonization and women began to speak up about their civil rights, in 1835, Halley's Comet again made its pass over the world. Its next approach, in 1910, was notable because it was the first comet to be photographed, and the first from which spectroscopic data was obtained. The comet made a close approach to Earth, which actually passed through its tail. It was a spectacular sight on May 19, 1910, although many were frightened because of an astronomer's incorrect prediction that its gas "would impregnate the atmosphere and possibly snuff out all life on the planet." This, of course, did not happen.

In China, the people believed for centuries that the comet indicated calamities, such as war, fire, pestilence, and a change of dynasty.

Astrologers are not so full of gloom and doom when this comet passes by, however. They do believe that with its release of gases that repressed emotions are released and that major social upheaval can occur. It's a shame that the women who protested for equality at Halley's 1835 appearance still didn't see a social change by the 1910 celestial visit. Sadly, Plath didn't stick around long enough to see the next one that would come in the Twentieth century, in 1986. But she did dream of comets:

> "Woke after a sleep & queer nightmare – of seeing a new comet or satellite – round, but conical, with the point behind it like a faceted diamond. I was up somewhere on a dark high place watching it pass over head like a diamond moon, moving rapidly out of sight & then, suddenly, three were a series of short sharp jerks & I saw the planet halted in a series of still-shot framed

exposures, which for some reason was a sight not granted to the human eye, & at once I was lifted, up, my stomach & face toward earth, as if hung perpendicular in mid-air of a room with a pole through my middle & someone twirling me about on it."

CHAPTER NINE

Sixth Mirror: The Arts and Humanities

Freedom!

"When archaeologists discover the missing arms of Venus de Milo, they will find she was wearing boxing gloves."
—John Barrymore, actor

When you think about the symbol for freedom in the United States, you think of the Statue of Liberty, a behemoth of a woman with a torch, modeled after that bright angel of many names whom you read about earlier. The Statue of Liberty stands near Ellis Island in New York, the immigration station at this U.S. port of entry. During the 19th-century wave of immigration, hundreds of thousands of men, women, and children made an unbearably long journey in ships across the Atlantic from Europe and Central Europe. The weary travelers disembarked to wait again in this holding station. There, they had to pass physical tests, provide documents, and register to become American citizens. Who were these people? If you are of European descent, probably your relatives, if your family emigrated from another country a few generations ago. What are the reasons for emigration? Freedom, opportunity, and escape from oppression and war, usually.

The story of immigration is as old as humanity itself: *Homo sapiens* left Africa some 75,000 years ago, for reasons unknown. The Bible tells of the lost tribes of Jews searching for their promised land. And just as Adam and Eve were exiled from the Garden of Eden, immigrants have been called for generations to risk death and suffering by leaving their homelands, by choice or by force. It's a story that never leaves the news, and sadly, might be more relevant than ever. By now, of course, you're seeing the correspondences with Plath's "Lady Lazarus." It's as much a poem about immigrants as it is about the abolitionists and suffragettes. It's about the promises of liberty and equality, which makes such perfect sense with this great female symbol of motherland carrying the torch.

The Statue of Liberty's actual full name is "Liberty Enlightening the World." While she is said to represent Libertas, the Roman goddess of freedom, her designer Bertholdi admitted that she was a composite of goddesses: Hera, wife of Zeus, with her similar face, clothing, sandals and torch; Venus, sometimes called Lucifer, or Isis; and Bertholdi's own mother. Liberty's original design had been submitted for construction in Egypt at the Suez Canal, but they were not interested. Bertholdi modified his drawings and presented "the same, identical woman" to the French as a gift of goodwill toward the United States.

Why might Plath have focused on the Statue of Liberty? She knew this statue well because she spent the summer of 1953 working in New York City before her breakdown and suicide attempt, events upon which her novel *The Bell Jar* is based. The

Statue of Liberty would have been the first thing Plath saw greeting her on return to her homeland after ocean-liner trips abroad, of which she took several. In 1957, Hughes commented on the "Statue of Lib" in a letter while he traveled with Plath. Of the Statue of Liberty, Plath wrote in her 1957 notebook: "irony: statue of own imprisonment in self, locks shut." Did Plath mean imprisonment in a woman's body? "Locks shut" certainly echoes her words "rocked shut" in "Lady Lazarus." Coming up, you'll see there are many more lines from her journal that seem to have inspired this poem.

In Plath's "Lady Lazarus," the Statue of Liberty is our narrator. From the first line, we hang onto her every word. She tells the tale of her unveiling and then recounts the trials and tribulations that she went through for it to happen. You saw back in Chapter Five, the History and the World mirror, that it was a pretty scandalous idea to design and make a giant copper-plated goddess at a time when public monuments were mostly statues of men. And this Lady's enormity was like none seen before, corresponding to Plath's question, "Do I terrify?"

She's a Ten

The purpose of the statue was to celebrate the Declaration of Independence's centennial. A centennial is not only a multiple of ten, but it is ten times ten and echoes the importance of the Plath poem's second line. The pedestal for the statue and the statue's dedication took place ten years after its first construction date. On the pedestal are lines from Emma Lazarus's sonnet, "The New Colossus." Each line of a sonnet has ten syllables, by the way.

While the statue was being assembled, her head and arm with its torch were exhibited separately. This corresponds with Plath's body parts in the eleventh stanza. The statue was a gift from France, but they had spent some righteous bucks and were hoping that the United States would kick in to jointly fund the project by paying for its pedestal. The year was 1875, the U.S. was fresh out of the Civil

War, and both Europe and North America were in an economic stagnation known as the "Long Depression." The pedestal problem almost halted all construction. In fact, for one reason or another, there seemed to be a financial crisis every ten years! That was the first trial, when Lady Liberty was ten years old, reflected in the twelfth stanza of "Lady Lazarus." After another decade, in 1885, it looked as if the statue project might "die" completely, reflected in Plath's thirteenth stanza. To complete the project a Pulitzer fundraising campaign "had to call and call" to solicit funds. Most donations were under one dollar and came from common citizens. We see the persistent requests in the fourteenth stanza until the fundraisers reached their goal.

As the completed statue towered over New York's harbor, New York City enjoyed its first ticker-tape parade, with a "million filaments" and its crowd "shoves in to see." A book from Plath's library on Yeats' spiritism,[27] *The Unicorn*, tells the story that in 1915, occultist Aleister Crowley paddled up the Hudson in a canoe, climbed the Statue of Liberty, and proclaimed the tiny island an Irish Republic. At the unveiling, the French flag was draped across her face. More than forty years later, in 1956, Hungarian nationalists hijacked the statue and put their flag across her. These drapes are now the napkin image Plath commands to be removed.

The original model of the Statue of Liberty stands at the Arts et Metiers Museum at the St. Martin des Champs Church in Paris, France.

---

[27] Spiritism is based on the five books of the Spiritist Codification by French writer Allan Kardec which document séances in which phenomena were observed that were attributed to incorporeal intelligence (spirits). Kardec sought to differentiate spiritualism and Spiritism. Spiritualism is common to various religions and is defined as the opposite of materialism. Kardec's work popularized talking (Ouija) boards, mesmerism, and other occult activities in the 1900s.

New York: Suffragette City

The Statue of Liberty was erected at the time that women were agitating for suffrage and women's rights. If you are of my era, or if you grew up watching old Disney musicals, you learned about suffragettes from the character of Mrs. Banks in the 1964 movie *Mary Poppins*. Plath mentions *Mary Poppins*, the book, several times in her journals and letters, so we know that she knew of the character Mrs. Banks. In the movie version, Mrs. Banks is more concerned with women's rights than with the happiness and welfare of her own children. Hollywood was clearly making its own statement about feminism in the early 1960s.

Plath's poem is full of female anger and vindication, as the statue was first displayed and erected in pieces. We see the limbs, the flames, and the huddled masses become Plath's "peanut-crunching crowd." In 1937, the Statue of Liberty was restored, her great "comeback." Her lights, previously blacked out for wartime, were again lit and were lit on victorious occasions such as D-Day, when she flashed the Morse code for victory. "A miracle!"

The Statue of Liberty has a classic Roman nose, blank eyes, and a crown with twenty-five rectangular windows, like the teeth described in Plath's fifth stanza. To walk up the Lady's spiral staircase to the crown might be considered a miracle of endurance. Her skin is made of bright copper sheets. Her right foot stands on a plaque like a great weight. Her critics and their "sour breath" were soon silenced.

By 1900, the statue's copper skin had taken on a green patina. There was fear of corrosion, that Plathian "grave cave" upon her. At this time, Lady Liberty was about thirty years beyond the time her construction had begun. In 1916, German saboteurs set off an explosion nearby, corresponding to the words "Nazi" and "Herr" throughout the poem. The statue sustained minor damage and was closed to the public, just as Plath's narrator shut down in "Lady Lazarus." There were also problems with lighting, addressing

Plath's filaments" image. A new generation of Pulitzers raised funds for exterior illumination.

Visitors to the statue must pay the cost, Plath's "charge," for the ferry across the water to Liberty Island. And of course, the ferry, which we saw mentioned earlier in an excerpt from Plath's letters, "really goes."

The flame of the torch on the statue is gold-plated like Plath's pure gold baby image. While the statue's copper has turned green, she still reflects the colors of sunrise, turning and burning. The broken shackles at Lady Liberty's feet represent freedom from oppression.

The Magic Number Seven

Designed and built by Freemasons, the Statue of Liberty has been called a "shrine to the number seven." Seven is important because of the seven Masonic liberal arts and sciences: grammar, rhetoric, dialectic, arithmetic, geometry, music and astronomy. Seven is a sacred number permeating aspects of every major religion, representing the seven seas, seven continents, the notes of the Western musical scale, the colors of the rainbow, days of the week, virtues and sins, sacraments and more.

Reflecting back, remember that The Lovers tarot card is the seventh card when counting from zero and it aligns with the seventh station on the Qabalah. That station, called *Netzach*, means "victory" and its symbol is fire. Netzach is assigned to Venus, according to *The Unicorn*. What is interesting is that the Statue of Liberty has seven rays emanating from her crown, and many numerical games are built into her dimensions. Lady Liberty's height and measurements have the curious addition of one inch added to seven feet, totaling 1813 inches, evenly divisible by seven 259 times. Adding 259 into itself (2+5+9) equals 16. This is no numerological accident. There are various instances of the number 16 (1+6) and the number 25 (2+5) which, when added together, also equal seven. This must be how freemason numerologists got their thrills.

Here is a good time to mention that Plath's "hand and foot" may also be seen as units of measurement. The hand, with beginnings in ancient Egypt and the Bible, is the traditional unit of measurement in Britain. Campbell wrote that the hand, qabalistically, has two sides, front and back. The word "Antichrist" reflects "anticheirist," meaning "contra-hand" and reflecting the devilishly female qlippoth. This is the root of the contemptuous remark, "The back of my hand to him."

Conspiracy theorists believe that the Statue of Liberty is a symbol of the Illuminati, a new world order secret society working through the masons in past centuries. Formed in Bavaria, a German state, in 1776, the Illuminati sought to abolish all monarchies, religion, private properties, and nation-states, to replace them with a utopia. Known as "the enlightened ones," they were the "hidden hand" in freemasonry, exemplified in portraits that showed their subjects hiding a hand inside a jacket. The most obvious Illuminati correlation is in Lady Liberty's original name, "Liberty Enlightening the World," and her radiant crown which represents enlightenment. The torch is held in the right hand, an Illuminati representation equating her with Prometheus and (surprise!) Lucifer. The Statue of Liberty is therefore actually a symbol of Lucifer, the "one who bears light." She is the planet Venus, the morning star, and Lucifer, as you now know, is regularly misinterpreted as a name for Satan.

> "Nations, races and individual men are unified by an image, or bundle of related images, symbolical or evocative of the state of mind, which is of all states of mind not impossible."
> —William Butler Yeats, from "Four Years," Part XXII

Okay, so you see a lot of connections between Lady Liberty and "Lady Lazarus." By this point, it's simply undeniable. And yet no one had ever seen them before now. It's all right in front of us, everything connecting to everything else on this liberty theme. But just in case that's not enough for you to say "Absolutely," here's more:

The Colossus of Rhodes

A long time ago, the Colossus of Rhodes, one of the seven wonders of the ancient World, was a giant statue of the Greek sun god Helios, erected between 292 and 280 B.C.E. Destroyed in an earthquake, it inspired the title poem for Plath's first book, *The Colossus and Other Poems*. In the 19th century, America's Statue of Liberty became "The New Colossus." Plath scholars have known that for a long time.

Here's where it gets fun: Consider the poem on the plaque at the base of the Statue of Liberty, titled "The New Colossus."

"The New Colossus" was written by the Russian-Jewish immigrant and feminist poet Emma Lazarus in 1883, to raise money for the pedestal. Plath borrowed much of her imagery from Emma Lazarus's sonnet:

"The New Colossus"

Not like the brazen giant of Greek fame,
With conquering limbs astride from land to land;
Here at our sea-washed, sunset gates shall stand
A mighty woman with a torch, whose flame
Is the imprisoned lightning, and her name
MOTHER OF EXILES. From her beacon-hand
Glows world-wide welcome; her mild eyes command
The air-bridged harbor that twin cities frame.

"Keep, ancient lands, your storied pomp!" cries she
With silent lips. "Give me your tired, your poor,
Your huddled masses yearning to breathe free,
The wretched refuse of your teeming shore.
Send these, the homeless, tempest-tost to me,
I lift my lamp beside the golden door!"

Emma Lazarus wrote "The New Colossus" after a trip to Europe, where she had witnessed firsthand the cruel persecution of Russian Jews. Lazarus also wrote the poems "Venus" and "Venus of the Louvre." The latter poem is about the German-Jewish poet Heinrich Heine (another *Herr*), who mourned his inability to love at the feet of Venus de Milo, "For vanished Hellas and Hebraic pain."[28]

Lazarus dedicated her first book of poems to her father, who had educated her at a time when women were often not educated. She idolized him, and it seemed that no one else could compare. As with Fuller, Plath might have also felt a kinship with Lazarus and the father worship.[29] Never marrying, Emma Lazarus kept social company with great writers such as Emerson and Browning and worked tirelessly for Jewish immigrant and abolitionist concerns. She died young, still in her thirties, having lived a brief, brilliant and fiery life. As Plath did too.

The Egyptian Book of the Dead

The Egyptian Book of the Dead was an important book for Plath's husband and mentioned in many of Plath's personal library books. Plath knew that author Joseph Campbell compared *Finnegans Wake* to this ancient text, a trippy soul-journey through a dreamlike landscape. In The Egyptian Book of the Dead, which is an ancient funerary text, Isis's titles read like crib notes for Emma Lazarus's poem. Some of her titles include *she who knows the orphan; she who seeks justice for the poor people; she who seeks shelter for the weak people; she who seeks the righteousness in her people*. Lazarus's poem "The New Colossus" is like Isis's bio if Isis were a poet getting introduced before a public reading.

So Plath paid tribute to suffragettes and especially to Emma Lazarus, who paid tribute to Isis represented as the Statue of

---

[28] *Hellas* is an ancient Greek name for Greece.
[29] See *Decoding Sylvia Plath's "Daddy": Discover the Layers of Meaning Beyond the Brute*, by Julia Gordon-Bramer (2017, Magi Press).

Liberty, who paid tribute to freedom in the likeness of a female goddess, who was a huge symbol for women's and immigrants' rights, who brings it back around again to Plath, who was a direct descendant of immigrants and the daughter of a suffragette. Got it?

The German "It"

How on earth can this poem contain any more meaning? That's a question I get asked again and again since I've been doing the *Decoding* work. I continue to be astounded by the power and depth of Plath's poems. I'll just keep presenting the facts here, and you have the opportunity to view them in context, check them, and convince yourself.

The country of Germany has touched Plath's poem "Lady Lazarus" in numerous ways. We have already seen Germanic-Norse mythology; the Germanic backgrounds of the Freemasons who built her; German saboteurs; the Passion Play; Nazi neopaganism; and finally, "Lady Lazarus" is the first *Ariel* poem in which Plath uses actual German words and specifically references the Nazis. You will see Nazis again both in the *Ariel* poems "Cut" and "Daddy," and more German is used in "Daddy." For Plath to use the German language is especially loaded in "Lady Lazarus," however, as the pronoun for a female is the English equivalent of "it."

Americans tend to think German's *Herr* is equivalent to *Mister*. That's not the case. The word *Herr* means *Lord*, implying the man is a master of something or someone. The word *Lady* holds no such power. In the old days, *Herren* (plural of *Herr*) were nobles, knights, masters, lords, rulers, bosses and gentlemen. *Herr* even accompanies titles for God (*Gott, der Herr*, meaning, *The Lord God*). Herr has built-in success, and you can be sure that is a masculine success.

Plath's repetition of *so* in "Lady Lazarus" means *that way* or *true* in both English and German. In German it can also mean "Is that so?" or "Is that a fact?" But "So-so," in addition to its Jewish and Stalinist associations explained earlier, has a different connotation: In English, the hyphenated "so-so" means mediocre or not good enough. Was Plath critical of *Herr Doktor*?

In his amusing 1880 essay, "The Awful German Language," author Mark Twain explains:

> "Every [German] noun has a gender, and there is no sense or system in the distribution; so the gender of each must be learned separately and by heart. There is no other way. To do this one has to have a memory like a memorandum-book. In German, a young lady has no sex, while a turnip has. Think what overwrought reverence that shows for the turnip, and what callous disrespect for the girl. See how it looks in print—I translate this from a conversation in one of the best of the German Sunday-school books:
>
> **Gretchen**. Wilhelm, where is the turnip?
>
> **Wilhelm**. She has gone to the kitchen.
>
> **Gretchen**. Where is the accomplished and beautiful English maiden?
>
> **Wilhelm**. It has gone to the opera."

Mark Twain was a Freemason, like Plath's father, belonging to the Polar Star Lodge No. 79 A.F. & A.M., in St. Louis. Twain's character appears frequently in James Joyce's *Finnegans Wake*. Along with his wife, Twain became involved and supportive of abolitionists and those fighting for women's rights and social equality. Twain was not a religious man, and wrote of Christianity as "a terrible religion." He did, however, believe in God, and stated his Qabalah-like acceptance that "the universe is governed by strict and immutable laws." In 1883, Twain was asked to contribute work to raise funds to build the pedestal to hold the Statue of Liberty. Twain sent a check and a letter to *The New York Times*, December 4, 1883, that included these words:

> "...suppose your statue represented her[:] old, bent, clothed in rags, downcast, shame-faced, with the insults and humiliation of

6,000 years, imploring a crust and an hour's rest for God's sake at our back door?—come, now you're shouting! That's the aspect of her which we need to be reminded of, lest we forget it."

In 1909, Twain said:

"I came in with Halley's Comet in 1835. It is coming again next year, and I expect to go out with it. It will be the greatest disappointment of my life if I don't go out with Halley's Comet. The Almighty has said, no doubt: Now here are these two unaccountable freaks; they came in together, they must go out together."

It is another fine connection with the fiery end of Plath's "Lady Lazarus," and the perfect match of The Lovers card to know that Twain did indeed go out with Halley's Comet.

Now, if you really want to drive yourself crazy with connections, check this out: "The New Colossus" was renamed "Give Me Your Tired, Your Poor," for a song in the 1949 Irving Berlin musical, *Miss Liberty*. Aside from the name Berlin hearkening to Germany, the play was about sculpting the Statue of Liberty, a symbol dear to the World War II soldiers coming home from the war. It is a play with themes of fame and scandal, the Pulitzers, and it even has a rich cast of characters known as "the Sharks." What are the chances?

Shine Little Glow-Worm, Glimmer

Glow little glow-worm, fly of fire
Glow like an incandescent wire
Glow for the female of the species
Turn on the AC and the DC
This night could use a little brightnin'
Light you up you little ol' bug of lightnin'
When you gotta glow, you gotta glow
Glow little glow-worm, glow
---Lyrics by the Mills Brothers, 1952

In another amusing yet relevant aside, Great Britain's legendary glow-worms are found in Devon, England, where

Plath and Hughes lived at the time she wrote "Lady Lazarus." The glow-worm also unbelievably correlates with the worms of the fourteenth stanza. Before you think I'm pushing it here, Plath mentioned, "Singing the glowworm song" in her 1957 poem "The Disquieting Muses," so we know she knew about them, and this song, long before she moved to Devon. In Devon, the glow-worms' numbers began to decline in the 1950s and 1960s, and to the region this was a really big deal. After all, these creatures are literary stars of the insect world, found in the works of writers such as Dryden, Hardy, and Tennyson. Shakespeare wrote that they evoked "ineffectual Fire" in *Hamlet*. Wordsworth called them "earth-born stars." But here's the thing: Only *female* glow-worms glow. Roald Dahl's 1961 story *James and the Giant Peach* features a six-legged (corresponding to that number on The Lovers card) female glow-worm, which provided light and ultimately saved the city of New York from an enormous electric bill by illuminating the Statue of Liberty's torch. New York! The Statue of Lib! Hell-o?!

Because this universe is such a complex place, and its qabalistic connections, like the galaxies, run in all directions for infinity, there are other artistic sources that may also have been inspirational for Plath when she wrote "Lady Lazarus," and these all tidily correspond to The Lovers card too.

I can practically hear you thinking, *I'm exhausted. What can't you fit into this poem?* But the fact is, not just any story can be worked in. It has to be exactly right and meet these qabalistic requirements. Plus, it has to be a work of art that we know or have pretty good reason to believe that Plath knew. So here we go:

We know that Plath owned and read a book called *Venus Observed* by English dramatist and poet Christopher Fry. It is a very Judgement of Paris-like story, where a duke who happens to love astronomy, brings three women home with the intention of marrying one of them.

Plath also probably read the classic novella, *Venus in Furs*, by Austrian author Leopold von Sacher-Masoch. The story is based on themes of female dominance and sadomasochism—here we go again. It begins with a man who dreams of speaking to the goddess Venus about love. At the end of the book, the protagonist declares:

> "That woman, as nature has created her, and man at present is educating her, is man's enemy. She can only be his slave or his despot, but never his companion. This she can become only when she has the same rights as he and is his equal in education and work."

Finnegans Wake

In another book in this series, *Decoding Sylvia Plath's "Daddy,"* we look at "The Freudian *Finnegans Wake*," an archetypal family drama in military-historical terms, constructed in a circular, womb-like design that starts and ends with the same words.

Finnegans Wake is considered to be James Joyce's masterpiece by many. As you have seen, we've referenced this work and Campbell's *A Skeleton Key to Finnegans Wake* all along as important books for Plath. Joyce substantially contributed to Plath's understanding of qabalistic structure and theory in literature. Plath's "Lady Lazarus" is full of references to this work. A dominant theme of *Finnegans Wake* is about revealing ALP, the great mother. The number ten is at its structural core, with footnotes to a count of ten. There are ten one-hundred letter words in the book. According to writer and Joyce scholar Peter Chrisp, Joyce's use of ten is said to represent the 10 Sephiroth, or stations, of the Kabbala. Elsewhere Joyce gives us "reechoable mirthpeals and general thumbnosery." Many symbols in *Finnegans Wake* are found in "Lady Lazarus," with Phoenix Park, Adam and Eve, Lucifer, St. Brigid, light-verus-darkness, the power of the "All-Mother," and even the fin idea is echoed in the appearances of *Huckleberry Finn* and legendary Irish giant, Finn MacCool. We saw in *Decoding Sylvia Plath's "Daddy"* that Plath underlined and starred this comment from the editorial introduction of her book on Joyce:

> "he evoked the past to illuminate the present."

Digging into Plath's work, this was clearly her intention too. Also in this book, she underlined parts about Jung's rational unconscious, collective myth, and the editor's statement,

> "Joyce has managed, by invoking an ancient myth, to conjure up a modern one."

I'm going to let Joseph Campbell sum up the experimental, spiritual novel *Finnegans Wake*, because, even though the language is sexist by our standards today, Campbell said it best:

> "Joyce early understood that unless we transcend every limitation of individual, national, racial, and hemispherical prejudice, our minds and hearts will not be opened to the full stature of Man Everlasting. Hence his zeal to shatter and amalgamate the many gods. Through the lineaments of local tradition he sends an X-ray, and on the fluorescent screen of *Finnegans Wake* projects the permanent architecture of all vision and life. For him Krsna *[Krishna]*, the Buddha, Osiris, Dionysus, Finn MacCool, the Christ, and Mohammed are substantially one; but one with these also, though unconscious of the fact, is the modern citizen of Dublin crossing the green of Phoenix Park. Beneath our constricting coats and vests we are Man the Hero, triumphant over the snares of life and over the sting of death, sublime behind the tailorings, the petty harryings, marryings, and buryings of the endless round in this valley of tears and joy.
>
> James Joyce did not subscribe to the journalistic fallacy that everything should be easy to understand. He knew that there are levels of experience and consciousness that can be reached only by a prodigious effort on the part of the creative artist, and comprehended only after a comparable effort on the part of the audience. Nietzsche's description of his own creative struggle, "I write in blood, I will be read in blood," is applicable tenfold to Joyce. *[...]* And now the great miracle occurs: even though the

race does not cerebrally grasp the full charge of the message, the artist's labor has not been in vain. A subtle radiance emanates from his work and seeps into the unconscious of his age."

That "subtle radiance," of course, is what Plath managed, even though everyone had missed the point for more than fifty years since her death.

Other Feminist Forerunners

At the beginning of this book, you saw a poem by Plath's friend, Anne Sexton, called, "The Hangman." It shares several key images with Plath's "Lady Lazarus." There was another poet just before Plath's time, who went by the initials H.D. (Hilda Doolittle). H.D. broke ground with an avant-garde imagist poetic voice. We know Plath owned at least two books with H.D.'s poetry. H.D. got much of her inspiration visiting the Print Room in the British Museum, examining Nishiki-e prints that incorporated traditional Japanese verse. She merged this influence with inspiration from Classical Greek literature, especially Sappho,[30] to find a style all her own.

H.D. lived in Bloomsbury, the district of London where Plath and Hughes were married. Plath no doubt walked past H.D.'s blue memorial plate at 44 Mecklenburgh Square many times. H.D. was close friends with another of Plath's literary idols, D.H. Lawrence (It does get confusing with all these initials). H.D. was an unapologetic feminist and bisexual, and the *FSGL* system has decoded Plath's July 1961 poem, "Finnesterre," to be in part Plath's tribute to H.D., composed at the time of the famous poet's death from a stroke.[31] In H.D.'s poem, "Helen," the color white represents the icy hatred and envy Greece had for the beautiful Helen of Troy. The same hands, knees, foot and ash imagery Plath uses in "Lady Lazarus" is here in this poem:

---

[30] Plath's cat was named "Sappho."
[31] The FSGL interpretation of "Finnesterre" has not been published at the time of this writing.

"Helen" By H. D.

All Greece hates
the still eyes in the white face,
the lustre as of olives
where she stands,
and the white hands.

All Greece reviles
the wan face when she smiles,
hating it deeper still
when it grows wan and white,
remembering past enchantments
and past ills.

Greece sees unmoved,
God's daughter, born of love,
the beauty of cool feet
and slenderest knees,
could love indeed the maid,
only if she were laid,
white ash amid funereal cypresses.

The mythic Helen of Troy "launch'd a thousand ships" with her beauty in the same way that the Statue of Liberty does today. Helen confronts Aphrodite in *Iliad*, accusing her of sexual envy.

So there's a great feminist, imagist poet H.D. with a poem that has all the same body parts (eyes, face, hands, knees, feet), face, smile, reflection on the past, ash, and of course, feminine sexuality and the idea of death. However, THE feminist forerunner for Plath was Virginia Woolf. Plath praised Woolf many times in journals and letters.[32] She wrote:

---

[32] Plath wrote in 1958: "I felt mystically that if I read Woolf, read Lawrence - (these two, why? - their vision, so different, is so like mine) - I can be itched and kindled to a great work: burgeoning, fat with the texture & substance of life: this my call, my work: this gives my being a name, a meaning: 'to make of the moment something permanent."

"Why did Virginia Woolf commit suicide? Or Sara Teasdale - or the other brilliant women - neurotic? Was their writing sublimation (oh horrible word) of deep, basic desires? If only I knew. If only I knew how high I could set my goals, my requirements for my life! I am in the position of a blind girl playing with a slide-ruler of values. I am now at the nadir of my calculating powers."

Woolf's *Mrs. Dalloway,* a feminist-themed novel published in 1925, *also* contains references to the bones, teeth, ash, and other elements in Plath's poem. Woolf wrote:

"...when London is a grass-grown path and all those hurrying along the pavement this Wednesday morning are but bones with a few wedding rings mixed up in their dust and the gold stoppings of innumerable decayed teeth."

Here's another one: Plath loved Nietzsche (called him "my boy neitzsche" [*sic*] and "my favorite philosopher"), and Nietzsche's *Thus Spake Zarathustra* was a seminal book for her. Looking into this, in "Lady Lazarus," we see the consumed-by-fire theme in Nietzsche's poem "Ecce Homo":

"Yes, I know from where I come!
Insatiable like the fire do I glow, consume myself.
Light is everything that I seize,
Ashes everything that I leave:
Fire am I without fail."

Nietzsche continues on about fire and ashes in *Thus Spake Zarathustra* when he speaks to the hermit on the mountain.

While we're on the subject of philosophers, let's throw this one out there as a possible inspiration: what about Søren Kierkegaard's *The Sickness Unto Death*? This was a book Plath owned and marked up heavily with underlinings and annotations. It's a work of Christian existentialism, named after the quote from the Lazarus story in the Gospel of John, 11:4: "This sickness is not unto death."

Finally, in Plath's December 1958 journals, she wrote notes after a particularly powerful session with her therapist, Dr. Ruth

Beuscher, who she had on another occasion referred to as "psychologist-priestess." This journal entry would not be relevant to the "Lady Lazarus" poem, except for the similar language and images in these six or so pages. Plath wrote that her father "heiled Hitler" at home. Of her selfless, doormat mother, she mocked her mother's words, writing, "I have ulcers, see how I bleed," which shares the same rhythm and feeling of "These are my hands / My knees." "Life was hell" conjures "I do it so it feels like hell." Plath's mother Aurelia had become her own Lazarus after Otto Plath's death.

Next, Plath said: "My mother killed the only man who'd love me steady through life." This becomes the man-eater of the last stanza. Her "I hated men because they didn't have to suffer like a woman did," echoes women's rights. Additionally, there are references to New York, and to Jews; to the "sticky white filth of desire" suggesting Plath's poetic sticky pearls (if you'll forgive me for getting graphic); to "Put her in a cell"; and to the symbol of stinking breath. Meanwhile, Plath expresses the pain of being expected to be perfect. Perhaps Aurelia Plath, the anti-role model, as a downtrodden, subservient woman at the hands of Sylvia Plath's authoritarian German father, has more to do with "Lady Lazarus" than we ever guessed.

The echoes are everywhere, the same symbols telling us the same story in all these different ways. The same story with different names, because we are living the myth, Joyce's repetitive structure, this eternal initiation that continues even today. Maybe you think it is all chance, despite the mathematics which suggest otherwise. That's cool. You're allowed. Hopefully you'll still see the connections. Or maybe you think Plath knew what she was doing with a qabalistic ordering. Even if she did know, was she aware of how many great works of alchemy, mythology, history, astronomy and astrology, art and literature had fed her creations? Did she truly understand the spell she would put upon us all?

CHAPTER NINE

Decoding Sylvia Plath's "Lady Lazarus" in the Classroom

Teaching Guide

Thank you for considering *Decoding Sylvia Plath's "Lady Lazarus"* for your classroom. This section is a guide for expanding upon Plath's poem "Lady Lazarus" for an interactive, stimulating and fun experience. This class plan may be adapted for traditional classrooms, online courses, and creative writing workshops, and it has been tested in actual classrooms for two years with great success.[33] Please feel free to modify this plan to suit your own unique needs, and please, please share your ideas and suggestions with the author at DecodingSylviaPlath@gmail.com.

For the last fifty years, Sylvia Plath has unfortunately been known more for her history of mental instability and tragic suicide than for her brilliance. There are two primary reasons for this: First, her single published novel, *The Bell Jar*, is continually and unfortunately read solely as autobiography. Secondly, Plath's poetry, especially the *Ariel* collection, opened up the new genre of confessional poetry and was, therefore, read also as autobiography. Readers interpret Plath's work literally regardless of her husband Ted Hughes's claims that hers was not confessional poetry, but rather a mystical work "of the highest tradition."

What my first book, *Fixed Stars Govern a Life: Decoding Sylvia Plath* set out to prove is that Plath was a great deal more than a depressive and unstable angry suicide and that her work is a great deal more than autobiography. Through *FSGL,* and this *Decoding Sylvia Plath* series, you will learn that each of Plath's poems is a synthesis of multiple perspectives contributing to a greater mystical structure and that Sylvia Plath was possibly the greatest genius in literature from the last hundred years.

Should you decide to work through the poems covered in *Fixed Stars Govern a Life: Decoding Sylvia Plath,* Volume One, you will

---

[33] Online courses using the *Fixed Stars Govern a Life: Decoding Sylvia Plath, Volume One* text (2014, Stephen F. Austin State University Press) at Lindenwood University's graduate creative-writing degree program, 2015-2017.

soon understand how one and all poems relate to the whole of the Qabalah Tree of Life. Check Amazon and other distributors for *Decoding* books and class plans for the first twenty-two poems in *Ariel,* for which *Decoding* books are forthcoming. Some copies of *FSGL* are still available online as well, although now it is out of print.

If you are exploring "Lady Lazarus" with your class without first reading *Fixed Stars Govern a Life,* you might want to peruse the introductory readings "What Set Me Going," "Author's Notes on How to Read these Interpretations," and "Understanding the Mirrors," that begin this program. These can be found online at no cost here: https://lindenwood.academia.edu/JuliaGordonBramer. It might be helpful to understand my process as to how I decoded "Lady Lazarus," because these findings are new and original at the time of this writing.

As an instructor, you might want to structure the first class around these introductory readings. This will help to familiarize students with the language, provide introductory images of the tarot and Qabalah Tree of Life (also found in the beginning section of *FSGL*), as well as offer biographical material on Sylvia Plath. Suggested supplemental materials follow, as does an appendix with a sample syllabus, student projects, and more. Smaller classes might be able to get through more information more quickly than large groups.

If the instructor is interested in focusing on the order of the *Ariel* poems, or on a poem's imagery and meaning within the corresponding tarot card, you can choose to bring in actual tarot cards, or simply project tarot card images on a screen. The tarot cards presented should be either the Rider-Waite or Universal Waite Tarot decks (the latter are colored more brightly), both featuring artwork by Pamela Colman Smith. The Rider-Waite Tarot was the deck that Ted Hughes most likely purchased for Plath's birthday in 1956, and the deck that Plath used, given its availability in England at the time and its strong correlation with the *Ariel* poems.

As an instructor, the availability of *FSGL* or other *Decoding Sylvia Plath* books, your amount of class time, the number of times the class meets, and the number of classes within a semester all figure into how many poems you decide to cover, as well as how many exercises and which ones you use.

This class plan is a living document, and I will continually be incorporating new ideas and sharing teaching methods that seem appropriate. In addition to sharing best practices on the *FSGL* website, www.fixedstarsgovernalife.com, please feel free to write me with your comments and ideas for improvement.

"And now you try
Your handful of notes;
The clear vowels rise like balloons."
—Sylvia Plath, "Morning Song"

Thank you,
Julia Gordon-Bramer

Suggested Supplemental Materials:

[Online courses might want to post these links]

Rider-Waite Tarot deck images may be found here: http://en.wikipedia.org/wiki/Rider-Waite_tarot_deck. The twenty-two major arcana cards correspond with Plath's first twenty-two poems in *Ariel*, as explained in *Fixed Stars Govern a Life*, Volume One.

The Rider-Waite and Universal Waite Tarot decks are available through U.S. Games. They can be found online, in many bookstores and occult shops, or on Amazon.com.

PBS *Voices and Visions* documentary about Sylvia Plath: https://www.youtube.com/watch?v=wmamNSa3sP8 (one hour)

Audio interview with Sylvia Plath: https://www.youtube.com/watch?v=g2lMsVpRh5c With Peter Orr of the British Council, 1962. (time: 14:10) The transcript may be read here:

http://www.english.illinois.edu/maps/poets/m_r/plath/orrinterview.htm.

A Skype interview with author Julia Gordon-Bramer may be scheduled at no cost with your class or book club to discuss the course material, Gordon-Bramer's personal experiences in decoding Plath, and more. Schedules permitting, this might include free tarot card readings for students.

Email: DecodingSylviaPlath@gmail.com for more information.

Recommended follow-up reading:

Fixed Stars Govern a Life: Decoding Sylvia Plath, Volume One by Julia Gordon-Bramer. 2014, Stephen F. Austin State University Press, or forthcoming *Decoding* books focusing on individual poems in *Ariel.*

Her Husband, by Diane Middlebrook. 2003, Penguin Books.

Wintering: A Novel of Sylvia Plath, by Kate Moses. 2003, Anchor Books.

Birthday Letters, by Ted Hughes. 1998, Farrar, Straus and Giroux.

Required Text:

Ariel: The Restored Edition, by Sylvia Plath, 2004, HarperCollins. (**Important:** any editions of *Ariel* before 2004 present the poems in a different order and are not suitable for understanding the *Fixed Stars Govern a Life* system.)

Decoding Sylvia Plath's "Lady Lazarus," by Julia Gordon-Bramer. 2017, Magi Press.

Key Goals and Benefits for Students from this Coursework:

- To demonstrate and create opportunities to teach inductive reasoning in both reading and writing.
- To understand the structure of the contemporary poem, and especially a Sylvia Plath poem.
- To understand, identify, and interpret symbolism in poetry.
- To be able to unpack a poem and discover the other various meanings and influences beneath a poem's literal and most superficial meaning.
- To expand students' reading and writing vocabulary.
- To gain an introductory knowledge of some of the more popular schools of mysticism and how they complement and inter-relate with other occult systems.
- To encourage students' creative expression.

Class Plan: *Decoding Sylvia Plath's "Lady Lazarus": Freedom's Feminine Fire*

Reading Assignment:

Students should read Plath's poem, "Lady Lazarus" on pages 14-17 of *Ariel: The Restored Edition* and *Decoding Sylvia Plath's "Lady Lazarus"* for the interpretation of this poem.

Class Warm-up Exercise:

As a group, discuss first impressions of Plath's poem "Lady Lazarus."

Instructor Notes:

"Lady Lazarus" is the poem that first comes to everyone's mind when Plath is described as suicidal. What most people do not understand is that it is the primary goal of mysticism (and even some religions like Buddhism) to kill the weak, impure human ego and undergo resurrection into a superior being of the spirit. Death of the ego and rebirth is the journey of Initiation. As symbolized in the Tarot, it begins with the Fool tarot card and ends with The World.

It is no coincidence that in viewing the connecting words, images, and themes across Plath's first seven *Ariel* poems, we see a quest for public image (fame) that leaves only emptiness. Also important to know is that in early October 1962, Plath received a copy of her friend Anne Sexton's collection of poetry, *All My Pretty Ones*, a week before beginning the infamous *Ariel* poems. In the book, Sexton plays with some of the same rhythms, dark tones, and dangerous suicidal musings. In this collection, Sexton equates women with Lucifer in her poem "Ghosts," and even uses Lazarus imagery in her poem, "The Hangman." Plath was obviously inspired by Sexton's image and tone when Plath wrote "Lady Lazarus."

Sylvia Plath grew up in America during World War II. As movies were a primary form of entertainment, she saw many newsreels about the war and she grew up learning that her family heritage represented the enemy. Plath's mother Aurelia was Austrian and her father Otto was German-Prussian. Therefore, "Lady Lazarus" is weighted with negative examples of German culture: The Nazi party and hints of their terrible crimes against humanity *[Nazi lampshades, paperweights, linen]*, and the sexist, paternalistic weight of the Deutsch language itself *["Herr Doktor"]*, which Plath struggled to learn into her young adult years. The German language surfaces again in her later *Ariel* poem, "Daddy": "Ich, ich, ich, ich / I could hardly speak. / I thought every German was you. / And the language obscene" (Plath, 74-75). When Plath was in high school, her class took a trip to Germany, in part to see the famous Passion Play in Oberammergau, Germany. Plath could not afford to join them.

In fall of 1959, Plath and Hughes stayed a few months at the Yaddo arts colony in New York State. They had returned to America from England the previous year by ship, passing the Statue of Liberty in the harbor at New York City. Plath wrote the title poem of her first book of poetry, "The Colossus," about the Colossus of Rhodes, one of the seven wonders of the ancient world. Plath's poem "The Colossus" is widely interpreted as a metaphor for the destruction of and piecing together of memories around her father, using this statue as a metaphor *[Instructors might want to visit this earlier Plath poem]*.

At the base of the Statue of Liberty is a poem, "The New Colossus," written by Jewish poet Emma Lazarus. Plath saw this statue of a grand feminine goddess as a transformative icon for the power of women, rooted in the goddess Isis and all of her incarnations around the world. "Lady Lazarus," therefore, became Plath's second Colossus poem: this time, a tribute to the new one, to women, and to her new self.

Teaching Tip:

"Lady Lazarus" is the first *Ariel* poem to specifically refer to Jews, a theme repeated in several Plath poems to follow. Remember also that Qabalah originated with Kabbalah—ancient Jewish mysticism.

Plath and Occult Vocabulary:

Students should each look up and note the definition of the following words, used throughout the text. [Online students should post these words in a Journal or similar function]:

- Initiation
- Qliphoth
- The Emerald Tablet
- Sacred
- Profane
- Annihilate
- Filaments
- Herr
- Doktor
- Opus
- Lucifer

In-Class Activity:

[Online classes may do this via discussion board.]

In small groups or as a whole class, have one student read "Lady Lazarus" aloud to the group. Next, have another student read it, attempting to present it in a different fashion. Have fun with it, and encourage the presenters to be as theatrical as they wish. Discuss and note differences in poetic delivery, inflection, and if any particular words or themes stood out with one person reading and not with another. Why or why not?

[Online: Students should read the poem aloud and record themselves. Suggest that another friend or family member read this too, for comparison. If sound files may be uploaded to school software, students might want to hear each other read this work. Some people have recorded themselves reading Plath's work on YouTube, and this too can be a source for different presentations]

Key Themes:

As a group, have students identify the most obvious themes: feminine power, anger, suicide. Write all themes on the board.

[Online: Post key themes on Discussion Board]

Emotional Content:

Is "Lady Lazarus" an angry poem? Why or why not?

Structure:

"Lady Lazarus" is one of Plath's longer poems, written in twenty-eight stanzas (28 is divisible by 7) of tercets (the maiden/mother/crone of Robert Graves's revered White Goddess?). Many lines in "Lady Lazarus" are seven syllables long. Knowing what you do from *FSGL* about the Statue of Liberty being called "a shrine to the number seven" (*FSGL* 59), do you believe there a qabalistic mirror in this structure?

Sounds:

What consonant and vowel sounds repeat throughout "Lady Lazarus"?

Discussion Questions:

1. Where, specifically, in "Lady Lazarus" are representations of feminism and feminist goddesses?

2. Does Plath cast herself as "Lady Lazarus" in this poem? Is it someone else?

3. Suicide is a subject in "Lady Lazarus," but the *Decoding* text explains that suicide is more of a metaphor. For what? Where is this metaphor in the poem?

4. How do repeated images connect the previous poem, "Barren Woman," with "Lady Lazarus"?

5. Can any connections be drawn from "Barren Woman" with the line, "I imagine myself" and the "Lady Lazarus" line "I manage it—"? Is this an example of the idea becoming a reality? Explain.

6. Might those who "injure me with attentions" (from "Barren Woman") be the same "peanut-crunching crowd" (from "Lady Lazarus"? Why or why not?

7. How do words like "So" affect the pace and tone of "Lady Lazarus"? Is this a kind of dismissal of male authority?

8. "Do not think I underestimate your great concern" reads like condescending mockery. What is this tone demanding from her reader? From society?

9. Show the story of the Statue of Liberty across the poem "Lady Lazarus."

10. Discuss the Jewish feminist immigrant poet Emma Lazarus, and how this poem reflects her.

Group Work and Discussion on the Mirrors:

Find examples of The Lovers tarot card and its qabalistic mirrors in "Lady Lazarus" *[death, resurrection, choice, passion, tests and trials, and so on]*

Find examples of the alchemical mirrors within the poem *[White and Black phases, burnings and dross, uniting opposites, and so on]*

Find the mythological mirrors within "Lady Lazarus" *[Aphrodite, Venus, Lucifer, Isis, Hesperus, and so on]*

Find the historical and world mirrors within "Lady Lazarus" *[German Neopaganism, Black Death, the Passion Play, the Lazarus Shark, Venus Fly Trap, Margaret Fuller, Lady Shark Fin, Statue of Liberty, and so on]*

Find the astrological and astronomical mirrors within "Lady Lazarus" *[Venus/Lucifer, solar filaments]*

Find the arts and humanities mirrors within "Lady Lazarus" *[The German language, "The New Colossus" by Emma Lazarus, Helen of Troy, Mrs. Dalloway, Finnegans Wake, and so on]*

Optional Exercises/Projects:

Dare to rewrite "Lady Lazarus" or another favorite Plath poem, but in your own words. Share with the class and describe the experience, whether successful or otherwise. What did you learn?

Most of Plath's poems begin *in medias res*—in the middle. Rarely does she set things up with an explanatory setting or information as to whom might be speaking. Play with this idea: Write a set-up for "Lady Lazarus, or another *Ariel* poem, and see what evolves. Share with the group.

Visually diagram key thematic connections (Gordon-Bramer's "mirrors") in "Lady Lazarus" with a mind-map. Encourage students to get as creative as they want either drawing by hand or using the computer.

Color/collage/illustrations are encouraged. Look online for examples or models of mind-maps.

The *Fixed Stars Govern A Life: Decoding Sylvia Plath* system, in summary:

Every poem in *Ariel* has six mirrors, reflecting the Qabalah's six-sided Tree of Life:

First: Tarot/Qabalah symbolism
Second: Alchemy
Third: Mythology
Fourth: Astronomy and Astrology
Fifth: History and World Events
Sixth: Arts and Humanities

Not only did Plath write one poem containing six perfect and different correspondences within the same set of words, but she did this *forty times* in *Ariel*—all in perfect relation to the tarot/Qabalah.

The poem "Lady Lazarus," and all Plath's *Ariel* poems, resonate with readers fifty years later because they include qabalistic subconscious touch-points. Readers don't have to understand it to feel it. It is a kind of a spell.

All facets work together to support the whole, creating enlightenment, paralleling the Qabalah's Tree of Life.

For more information, email: DecodingSylviaPlath@gmail.com.

> "And above all, watch with glittering eyes the whole world around you because the greatest secrets are always hidden in the most unlikely places. Those who don't believe in magic will never find it."
> —Roald Dahl

Bibliography

Abraham, Lyndy. *A Dictionary of Alchemical Imagery.* Cambridge, UK: Cambridge University Press, 1998. Print. p. 106.

Alexander, Paul, editor. *Ariel Ascending: Writings about Sylvia Plath.* 1985. Harper and Row: New York.

Alvarez, A. "How Black Magic Killed Sylvia Plath" for *The Guardian.* 14 September, 1999. Web. https://www.theguardian.com/theguardian/1999/sep/15/features11.g2 4 October 2017.

Alvarez, A. "Sylvia Plath: A Memoir" *Ariel Ascending: Writings about Sylvia Plath.* 1985. Harper and Row.

Allen, Richard Hinckley. *Star Names: Their Lore and Meaning* reprinted from Dover edition, 1963. Web. 3 October 2010.

American Heritage Magazine "Humanity, said Edgar Allan Poe, is divided into Men, Women, and Margaret Fuller" as quoted by Joseph Jay Deiss. August 1972. Web. http://www.biographyonline.net/women/margaret-fuller.html 5 October 2017.

Atlantic Monthly, July 19, 1962. "Geisha girl Harukoma (Etsuke's professional name) applies the white make-up that marks the Geisha as she prepares for an evening party with business executives, on July 19, 1962."

Babcock, Barbara."Taking Liberties, Writing from the Margins and Doing it with a Difference." *The Journal of American Folklore.* Vol. 100, No. 398, Folklore and Feminism (Oct.-Dec. 1987), pp. 390-411.

Baender, Paul (editor) Twain, Mark, *What is Man?: and Other Philosophical Writings.* 1973. University of California Press.

Bang, Mary Jo. "The Mythic Love Poem: Where white-hot sexuality and white-hot hatred meet." Slate.com. September 25, 2012. Web. http://www.slate.com/articles/arts/classic_poems/2012/09/the_mythic

_love_poem_where_white_hot_sexuality_and_white_hot_hatred_meet_.html. 02 October, 2012.

BeliefNet. "Lucifer: Satan, or Venus?" by Lynn Hayes. Web. http://www.beliefnet.com/columnists/astrologicalmusings/2009/07/lucifer-satan-or-venus.html. 5 October 2017.

Benet, William Rose and Conrad Aiken. *An Anthology of Famous English and American Poetry*. 1945. The Modern Library: New York. Sylvia Plath's copy is held in the Sylvia Plath archives in the Lilly Library at Indiana University-Bloomington.

Blanchard, Paula. *Margaret Fuller: From Transcendentalism to Revolution*. Reading, Massachusetts: 1987. Addison-Wesley Publishing Company.

Bloom, Harold. *Kabbalah and Criticism*. 1981. New York: Continuum.

Brad Meltzer's Decoded. "Statue of Liberty." 2011. *The History Channel website*. Episode 3, Season One. First aired December 10, 2010. http://www.history.com/shows/brad-meltzers-decoded/episodes/episodes-guide

Brodie, Fawn M. *No Man Knows My History: The Life of Joseph Smith*. 1945. Alfred A. Knopf. We know Plath read this book in 1948 for paper written for an English class.

Campbell, Joseph. *A Skeleton Key to Finnegans Wake: Unlocking James Joyce's Masterwork*. 1944. New World Library. Print. Plath's letters indicate she was reading this book on July 5, 1954 (*LSP*, 780).

Carson, Rachel. *The Sea Around Us*. We do not know the edition Plath read. She mentioned reading this in a letter to her mother on July 10, 1958. Carson's friend Val Gendron mentored Plath with writing exercises for a time in summer of 1952 (*LH*, 92).

Carson, Rachel. *Under the Sea-Wind*. New American Library. New York. 1941. Plath mentioned, in a letter to her mother on July 10, 1958, that Ted Hughes was reading this book. It is possible Plath read this book too.

Chase, Evelyn Hyman. *Feminist Convert: A Portrait of Mary Ellen Chase*. 1989. John Daniel and Co.

Chrisp, Peter. "From Swerve of Shore to Bend of Bay" Web. http://peterchrisp.blogspot.com/2014/04/our-drawings-on-line.html. 1 October, 2017.

Cousteau, Jacques-Yves and Frederic Dumas. *The Silent World: A Story of Undersea Discovery and Adventure.* Edited by James Dugan. Harper & Brothers Publishers, New York. 1953. We do not know which edition Plath read. In Plath's *Collected Poems*, Ted Hughes has a note that this book inspired "Full Fathom Five" (*CP*, 287).

Connors, Kathleen and Sally Bayley (editors). *Eye Rhymes: Sylvia Plath's Art of the Visual.* 2007. Oxford University Press.

Cooper, David. A. *God is a Verb*, New York: Riverhead Books. 1997.

Dahl, Roald. *James and the Giant Peach.* 1961. Alfred A. Knopf: U.K.

Darwin, Charles. *Insectivorous plants.* New York: D. Appleton and Company, 1875. Web. http://darwin-online.org.uk/EditorialIntroductions/Freeman_InsectivorousPlants.html 23 February 2011.

Gaither, Carl C. Alma E. Cavazos-Gaither. *Gaither's Dictionary of Scientific Quotations.* 2008. Springer Science and Business Media. Statement by Edmond Halley for *The Elements of Astronomy, Physical and Geometrical.* "A Synopsis of the Astronomy of Comets,"Volume 2, 1715. Printed for John Morphew, London, England.

Fatout, Paul. *Mark Twain Speaks for Himself* by Mark Twain, and "Letter to the Editor, *The New York Times*, December 4, 1883, by Mark Twain." 1997. Purdue University Press, pp. 135-136.

Fishbase.org. "*Etmopterus Lucifer* Jordan & Snyder, 1902 Blackbelly lanternshark" Web. http://www.fishbase.org/summary/Etmopterus-lucifer.html 5 October 2017.

Frege, Gottlob. 1892. "On Sense and Reference" as quoted in *Philosophy of Language: The Classics Explained* by Colin McGinn. 2015. MIT Press.

Frazer, Sir James George. *The Golden Bough: A Study in Magic and Religion.* 2009 Oxford World's Classics. New York.

Fuller, Henry James. *College Botany.* 1949. H. Holt and Company: New York. Plath owned this book and underlined parts of it.

Gilbert, D. T. (1998). "Speeding with Ned: A personal view of the correspondence bias" (PDF). In Darley, J. M.; Cooper, J. *Attribution and social interaction: The legacy of E. E. Jones.* Washington, D.C.: APA Press.

Goodwin, Joscelyn (Translator). *The Chemical Wedding of Christian Rosenkreutz* (Magnum Opus Hermetic Sourceworks Series: No. 18). With Introduction by Adam McLean. 1991. Phanes Press.

Gordon-Bramer, Julia. *Fixed Stars Govern a Life: Decoding Sylvia Plath*, Volume One. 2013. Stephen F. Austin State University Press.

Graves, Robert. *The White Goddess: a historical grammar of poetic myth.* 1948. Farrar, Straus and Giroux, New York.

Gray, Eden. *The Complete Guide to the Tarot.* Bantam; new edition 1982.

Greer, Mary K. *TV & Movie Tarot Watch List.* Web. https://marykgreer.com/2008/10/21/tv-movie-tarot-watch-list/. 5 October 2017.

Hogan, Kevin. Psy.D. *Covert Hypnosis. An Operator's Manual.* 2000. Network 3000.

Hughes, Ted. *Letters of,* selected and edited by Christopher Reid. 2002. Farrar, Straus and Giroux.

The Independent. "The great Gloucestershire glow-worm hunt" by Cole Moreton. Sunday, August 11, 1996. Web. http://www.independent.co.uk/news/uk/home-news/the-great-gloucestershire-glowworm-hunt-1309177.html Last accessed 25 June 2012.

Jacoby, Susan. *Freethinkers: a history of American secularism.* 2005. New York: Metropolitan/Owl.

Jewish Encyclopedia. "Frank, Jacob, and the Frankists" by Herman Rosental, S.M. Dubnow. Web. http://www.jewishencyclopedia.com/articles/6279-frank-jacob-and-the-frankists 5 October 2017.

Jewish Virtual Library. "Frank, Eva". http://www.jewishvirtuallibrary.org/jsource/judaica/ejud_0002_0007_0_06690.html Web. Last accessed 27 April, 2012.

Joyce, James. *The Portable James Joyce*. With an introduction and notes by Harry Levin. 1946. The Viking Press. This is the edition Plath owned and underlined and annotated. It can be found in the Sylvia Plath archives at the Lilly Library at Indiana University-Bloomington.

Katchen, Martin. "The Deepening Rift in American Judaism and the Turn Toward Revisionist Zionism." Political Theology Today. 06 December, 2016. Web. http://www.politicaltheology.com/blog/the-deepening-rift-in-american-jewry-and-the-turn-toward-revisionist-zionism-martin-katchen/

Khan, Yasmin Sabina. *Enlightening the World: The Creation of the Statue of Liberty*. 2010. Ithaca, New York: Cornell University Press.

Kierkegaard, Søren. *The Sickness Unto Death*. 1949. Princeton University Press. From Sylvia Plath's library, with numerous underlinings and annotations by Sylvia Plath (LibraryThing).

Langdon-Davies, John. *A Short History of Women*. 1927. Viking Press: New York.

Langer, Suzanne K. *Philosophy in a New Key: A Study in the Symbolism of Reason, Rite, and Art*. 1951. The New American Library: New York. From the personal library of Sylvia Plath. Some underlining and notes in margins. (LibraryThing) Web. https://archive.org/stream/pdfy-rhrw7VPajPHIhLwH/Philosophy%20in%20a%20New%20Key,%20Suzanne%20K.%20Langer_djvu.txt 5 October 2017

LibraryThing. "Legacy Library: Sylvia Plath." "Religion". Note: In addition to books specifically on Judaism, the Hebrew faith, and Jewish heritage and culture, Plath had many books on Mormonism.

There is a strong connection between the Mormon faith and Kabbalah (and therefore Judaism). Web. http://www.librarything.com/catalog/SylviaPlathLibrary&deepsearch= Religion 5 October, 2017.

LibraryThing. "Legacy Library: Sylvia Plath." "Unitarian" Plath had many books on the subject of her church.

Mann, Thomas. "Freud and the Future" for *Daedalus*. Vol. 88, No. 2 Myth and Mythmaking (Spring, 1959), pp. 374-378.

Lutzer, Erwin W. *God's Devil: The Incredible Story of Satan's Rebellion Serves God's Purpose*. 2015. Moody Publishers.

Middlebrook, Diane. *Her Husband: Ted Hughes & Sylvia Plath*. Penguin Books. New York, NY. 2003.

Milbrath, Susan. *Star gods of the Maya: astronomy in art, folklore, and calendars*. University of Texas Press, 1999.

Mill, John Stuart. *On Liberty*. 1947. Appleton-Century-Crofts: New York. From the Library of Sylvia Plath. Pencil sketch by Plath on the half-title page and extensive annotations throughout the book (LibraryThing). Much on "The Subjection of Women" and slavery. Web. https://www.gutenberg.org/files/34901/34901-h/34901-h.htm 5 October 2017

Moore, Virginia. *The Unicorn: William Butler Yeats' Search for Reality*. The Macmillan Company. New York. 1954.

Nietzsche, Friedrich. *Thus Spake Zarathustra*: A Book for All and None. 1891. Ernst Schmeitzner: Germany.

News.com.au "Diving in the bubbles of the coolest man on earth" Web. http://www.news.com.au/entertainment/tv/diving-in-the-bubbles-of-the-coolest-man-on-earth/news-story/53d70416e30ebf1fe545059bda100296 5 October 2017.

Oesterreich, T.K. *Possession—Demoniacal & Other: Among Primitive Races in Antiquity, the Middle Ages, and Modern Times*. We do not know the actual edition Plath read, but she mentioned it in her August 27, 1958 journal entry, on page 415 of *The Unabridged Journals of Sylvia Plath*. Contains information about the "South American Indians" (p. 257) and "the half-civilized peoples of ancient

America" (p. 292). We would consider this book both racist and sexist by today's standards. (LibraryThing)

Orr, Peter. "A 1962 Sylvia Plath Interview with Peter Orr." *Modern American Poetry.* http://www.english.illinois.edu/maps/poets/m_r/plath/orrinterview.htm Web. Last accessed 4 October 2017.

Owens, Lance. "Joseph Smith and Kabbalah: The Occult Connection." Web. http://gnosis.org/jskabb1.htm 5 October 2017

PBS NewsHour (July 7, 2010). "Mark Twain's Autobiography Set for Unveiling, a Century After His Death." Web. Last accessed: June 25, 2012.

Peel, Robin. *Writing Back: Sylvia Plath and Cold War Politics.* 2002. Rosemont Publishing.

Plath, Sylvia. *Ariel: The Restored Edition.* Foreword by Frieda Hughes. New York: HarperPerennial. 2004. "Lady Lazarus pp. 14-17. Introductions for the BBC: pp. 74-76. Print.

Plath, Sylvia. *The Collected Poems.* Ed. by Ted Hughes. 2008. New York: Harper Perennial Modern Classics. Print.

Plath, Sylvia. *Letters Home.* Selected and Edited with Commentary by Aurelia Schober Plath. 1975. HarperPerennial: New York. Print.

Plath, Sylvia. *The Letters of Sylvia Plath. Volume One: 1940-1956.* Ed. by Peter K. Steinberg and Karen V. Kukil. 2017. Faber and Faber. Print.

Plath, Sylvia. *The Unabridged Journals of Sylvia Plath.* Ed. by Karen V. Kukil. New York: Anchor Books, 2000. Print.

Plato. *The Timaeus of Plato.* Translated by Benjamin Jowett. Web. http://classics.mit.edu/Plato/timaeus.html 5 October 2017.

PRI. "Gagaku: Japanese Imperial Court Music" Web. https://www.pri.org/stories/2012-09-27/gagaku-japanese-imperial-court-music 5 October 2017.

Rákóczi, Basil Ivan. *The Painted Caravan: a penetration into the secrets of the tarot cards.* 1954, L.J.C. Boucher, The Hague. Print.

Radin, Paul (Editor). *African Folktales.* New York: Schocken Books. 1952. Print.

Reynolds, George. *The Story of the Book of Mormon*. 1888. Jos. Hyrum Parry. Web. https://books.google.com/books?id=VGEyqv_vsX4C&dq=The+story+of+the+Book+of+Mormon+by+George+Reynolds&source=gbs_nav links_s 5 October 2017.

Roob, Alexander. *The Hermetic Cabinet: Alchemy & Mysticism*. New York: Taschen. 2009. Print.

Rosicrucian text: *The Chymical Wedding of Christian Rosenkreutz*. 1459. http://zebratta.com/cwcr.htm Web. Last accessed 26 January 2011.

Sagan, Carl. *Cosmos*. 1980 Random House: New York Web. https://archive.org/stream/Cosmos-CarlSagan/cosmos-sagan_djvu.txt October 2, 2017.

Sacher-Masoch, Leopold von. *Venus in Furs*. Translated by Fernanda Savage. Originally published 1870. Project Gutenberg. Web. http://www.gutenberg.org/cache/epub/6852/pg6852.txt Last accessed 4 October 2017.

Scholem, Gershom. *Zohar: The Book of Splendor. Basic Readings from the Kabbalah*. Schocken Books: New York. 1949.

Sexton, Anne. *The Complete Poems of Anne Sexton*. First Mariner Books Edition. Houghton Mifflin Company, New York. 1999. From *All My Pretty Ones*. "The Hangman." p. 69.

Sharman-Burke, Juliet and Liz Greene. *The Mythic Tarot*. New York: Simon and Schuster. 1986. Print.

Slater, Abby. *In Search of Margaret Fuller*. New York: Delacorte Press, 1978

Smithsonian Magazine, "Alchemy May Not Have Been the Pseudoscience We All Thought It Was" by Richard Conniff. February 2014. http://www.smithsonianmag.com/history/alchemy-may-not-been-pseudoscience-we-thought-it-was-180949430/. Last accessed 15 September 2017.

Sojourner Truth Memorial. Web. http://sojournertruthmemorial.org/

Stanton, Elizabeth C., Susan B. Anthony, and Matilda J. Gage. *History of Woman Suffrage, vol. 1.* 1887. Rochester, NY: Charles Mann.

Stevenson, Anne. *Bitter Fame: A Life of Sylvia Plath.* New York: Penguin Books. 1998. Print.

Twain, Mark Twain, Mark. *A Tramp Abroad.* "That Awful German Language." Appendix D. 1880. American Publishing Company. Web: http://www.cs.utah.edu/~gback/awfgrmlg.html Web. Last accessed 24 January 2011.

Untermeyer, Louis. *Modern American Poetry, Modern British Poetry: a critical anthology.* 1942. Harcourt, Brace and Company. New York.

United States Bureau of the Census. *Census of Religious Bodies, 1936.* Washington: U.S. G.P.O., 1939-1940. Plath read "Unitarianism" in Vol. 2, Part 2 for her Religion 14 class. She used this in a school paper dated December 8, 1951 (per LibraryThing).

Vaillant, George C. *Aztecs of Mexico: Origin, Rise and Fall of the Aztec Nation.* Penguin Books. 1955. The actual edition read by Plath is unknown (LibraryThing). In a letter to her brother Warren on June 25, 1958, Plath mentioned reading a book on Aztecs and anthropology. In her journal entry July 3, 1958, she wrote: "My life is in my hands. I'm plowing through penguin books on Aztecs, the personality of animals, Man & the Vertebrates" (p. 399). This book covers other Mexican Indian cultures as well as Aztec.

Voices and Visions. "Sylvia Plath" Directed and Produced by Lawrence Pitkethly. ©1988 Annenberg Foundation. Film.

Waite, A.E. *The Hidden Church of the Holy Grail.* 1909. Author A.E. Waite is a co-creator of the Rider-Waite Tarot deck that Plath most likely used. Plath read this book for a course in medieval literature in 1952-1953. It includes very specific instructions for Hermeticism, Freemasony, the journey of Initiation, alchemical rites, Qabalistic ceremony and more. Web. http://www.sacred-texts.com/sro/hchg/pageidx.htm 5 October 2017.

Williams, Tennessee. *Suddenly Last Summer*. 1958. York Playhouse, New York.

Wilson, Andrew. *Mad Girl's Love Song: Sylvia Plath and Life before Ted*. New York: Scribner, 2013.

Woolf, Virginia. *The Voyage Out*. 1949. The Hogarth Press, London. Owned by Sylvia Plath (LibraryThing). A fictional story about women's suffrage and colonialism which takes place on a mythical voyage in South America.

Woolf, Virginia. *Mrs. Dalloway*. 1954. The Hogarth Press, London. Owned by Sylvia Plath (LibraryThing). Underlining and annotations throughout.

Specific References by Section:

Abbreviations:
UJ = *The Unabridged Journals of Sylvia Plath*
CP = *The Collected Poems of Sylvia Plath*
Letters = *Letters Home by Sylvia Plath*
LSP = *The Letters of Sylvia Plath, Volume 1*

What You Should Know Going In
"Your daughter shall start…" (*Letters*, 280)
"The modern woman…" (*UJ*, 452)
"Fundamental Attribution Error" (Gilbert)

Chapter Two: About the Poem "Lady Lazarus"
"The Hangman" (Sexton, 69)
"Passion Play in Oberammergau, Germany" (Wilson, 83) (*LSP*, 160)
"Plath had noticed and written of this statue" (*LSP*, 718)
"Sylvia's poems & novel hit…" (Hughes, 719)
"Hughes explained about the *Ariel*" (Hughes, 568)
"…The speaker is a woman…" (*Ariel*, 196)

The Structure of a Spell
"Hypnosis in the written and spoken word" (Brodie)
"Hughes coached Plath" (Hughes, 50)
"written for the ear…" (*Ariel*, 195)
"…whatever lucidity they may have…" (Middlebrook, 200)
"That's a hypnotic technique…" (Hughes, 445)

Discovering the Connections
"Perception is 9/10 of the law…" (Hogan, 13)
"Barren Woman" (*Ariel*, 13)
"Tulips" (*Ariel*, 18-20)

Chapter Three: First Mirror: Tarot and Qabalah
"I must meantime this June…" (*Journals*, 327)
Quote about "Dirge in Three Parts" (*LSP*, 681)
"The Mormon Church and the occult, Kabbalah…" (Owens)

Mormonism (LibraryThing)

"The Zohar discusses the universe…" (Cooper, 34)

"The Munich Mannequins" (*CP*, 262)

Why Would Plath Hide the Occult?

"the books in her library…" For detail on specific occult terms, ritual and ceremony, see especially *The Unicorn* (Moore); *The Golden Bough* (Frazer); *The White Goddess* (Graves); *The Hidden Church of the Holy Grail* (Waite); and her many books on Mormonism and religion, which are listed on LibraryThing.com.

"Hollywood movies use…" (Greer)

But wait! Sylvia Plath didn't believe in God…

"How Black Magic Killed Sylvia Plath." (Alvarez)

Unitarianism (LibraryThing)

About Plath's "Jew" References

"I began to talk like a Jew…" (*Ariel*, 75)

books on religion (LibraryThing)

Lilith, the Fiery Goddess

"Being born a woman…" (*UJ*, 77)

"About the book, she said" (*LSP*, 1306)

Where is The Lovers card in "Lady Lazarus"?

"So it seems very clear…" (Hughes, 568)

Qlipoth (Moore, 141-142, 219)

"God saw that it was necessary…" (Scholem, 4)

"Kabbalah is nothing if not sexist." (Bloom, 9)

"Ten is a milestone" (Gray, 188)

"Remember the old Bible story…" (John 11: 1-44)

Chapter Four: Second Mirror: Alchemy

Alchemy in the Mormon faith (Owens, part 2)

"The Unicorn…" (Moore, 112, 113, 180, 295, 297-300)

"Yeats' own take on in alchemy" (Moore, 41)

"…Frustrated? Yes." (*UJ*, 45)

"All of these details…" (Moore, 153)

"When Ted and I begin living together…" (*Letters*, 280)

"The horror of the academic writer…" (*Letters*, 342)

"...about her recent incident..." (Alexander, 196)
"from sea-foam" and "deep-sea daughter" (Campbell, 153, 234)
"shrub of liberty" (Campbell, 309)
"The Fall of Man" (Campbell, 193)
Red-haired men (Frazer, 439, 441, 514, 551-552)
"And the Lord God said, 'The man has now become like one of us, knowing good and evil" (Genesis: 3:22)
"like pearls" and "the grave" (Abraham, 77)
"stay put" (Abraham, 31)
"theatre" (Abraham, 199)
"hair and blood" (Abraham, 84)
"opposing forces" (Abraham, 141)
Rubedo (Abraham, 96)
"Plath's own books tell us that red hair..." (Frazer, 439, 441, 514, 531-552)

Third Mirror: Mythology

"I'm Your Venus". Song lyrics by Robbie van Leeuwen for the Dutch rock band Shocking Blue, 1969. Pink Elephant Records.
"Myth is the foundation of life..." (Mann, 371)
"The Chymical Wedding of Christian Rosenkreutz" (Goodwin)
"maiden, mother and crone" (Graves, 257)

Meet Venus/Aphrodite

"Here lies buried Lady Venus" (Goodwin)
Venus as Aphrodite (Frazer, 6, 8, 9)
"Listen to the mocking temptress" (Campbell, 158)

Meet Lucifer/Isis

Goddess (Graves, 73, 102, 198, 220, 232)
Many names (Frazer, 387-389)
"where the King of Tyre" (Lutzer)
Isis, the fertile mother (Langdon-Davies, 149)
Isis, the queen (Langron-Davies, 148, 150)

Meet the First Females: Lilith and Eve

Eve as Isis (Campbell, 9)

Meet Hecate/Brigit/Hera

Hecate (Langdon-Davies, 150)
Brigit (Frazer, 156) (Moore, 38, 71-72, 79)
Brigit/Bridget (Campbell, 26-27)
Hera (Claerr) (Frazer, 163-166) (Moore, 377, 383)

Meet Bast/Frige

"She had wrapped her marble-like body in a huge fur…" (Sacher-Masoch)

Cats (Frazer, 36, 82-83, 525-526, 707, 760-762, 785-786, 801)
Frigg (Frazer, 704)
Ra, connected to Isis (Frazer, 303)

Meet G-1 and Lady Shark Fin

Pre-Columbian Mixtec (*LSP*, 965)
"Mystic Mountain of Abiegnus" (Moore, 208)
Aztec gods in *The Story of the Book of Mormon* (Reynolds, 37, 44, 45)
"25-page thesis on Mormonism" (*LSP*, 140)
Ancient Mexican gods, Mexican history (Frazer, 32, 46, 91, 101, 120, 441, 500-501, 566, 569, 680-686, 790)
"9 Ik with 9 Wind." (Milbrath, 205)
"woman in early Mesoamerica" (Vaillant)
gods of primitive cultures (Oesterrich)
Quetzalcoatl (Frazer, 508, 610-11, 781)
Selden Rodman (*UJ*, 408)

Possible inspiration also from *The Voyage Out* (Woolf). This is a book Plath read and owned. Held at Smith College.

Fourth Mirror: History and World Events

"I find myself being more and more fascinated…" (Orr)
Women worshiped by ancient Germans (Frazer, 112)
Neopaganism (Frazer, 45, 48-49, 51, 112, 127, 137, 143, 186, 211, 272-273, 463, 466-467, 474, 494-495, 519-521, 522-523, 525-527, 530-535, 709, 712, 721-722, 738, 743, 767, 814, 771, 779-780, 791)
Census (US)

The Passion Play

"I started writing this play twelve years ago…" Ruhl. "Notes on *Passion Play.*" Web. http://www.sarahruhlplaywright.com/plays/view/PASSION-PLAY/ 4 October 2017.

"…one should be able to manipulate these experiences…" (Orr)

Cats, during Plague (Frazer, 760)

Just When You Thought It Was Safe To Go Back In The Water

Sharks (Cousteau)

"the Lazarus Shark of the Great Barrier Reef…" (News.com.au)

"the Lucifer Shark" (fishbase.org)

Sharks (Carson)

The Venus Flytrap

"The Venus flytrap, a devouring organism…" (Williams)

"her College Botany book" (Fuller, 233)

The Statue of Liberty

"no true patriot can countenance…" (Khan, 160)

"…if Liberty got down off her pedestal, she would not have been allowed to vote in either France or America" (Babcock, 401).

Margaret Fuller and Feminism

"held particular significance for her" (*LH*, 32)

Mary Ellen Chase (Chase)

"I am growing and…" (*LH*, 234)

Isis magazine (Peel, 149)

"to realize that most American males…" (*UJ*, 36)

"the great-granddaughter of Julia Ward Howe" (UJ, 489, 697)

Lucretia Mott (Jacoby, 95)

"I think that is why there are so many women's…" (UJ, 100)

"I am too fiery" (American Heritage)

"numerous biographies written about Fuller":

Margaret Fuller: Whetstone of Genius, by Mason Wade, 1940. Viking Press

Margaret Fuller by Julia Ward Howe, 1889 WH Allen & Co.

Margaret Fuller: a Psychological Biography by Katharine Susan Anthony, 1920. Jonathan Cape Publishers: London

"My father's image…" (Blanchard, 93)

"her early death" (Slater, 2-3)

Sojourner Truth

"Plath knew that since ancient Greece" (Langdon-Davies, 146-195)

Sojourner Truth's "Ain't I a Woman" speech (Sojourner)

"If the first woman God ever made…" (Stanton, 116)

On Liberty, women and slaves (Mill)

The Japanese Woman

"Wake from death and return to life." Web. http://www.linguanaut.com/japanese_sayings.htm 4 October 2017

"Plath read about Japanese culture and Geisha" (*Atlantic*, July 1962)

American films (*UJ*, 522)

"Gagaku Japanese Dancers" (*UJ*, 499)

Gagaku: Japanese Imperial Court Music (PRI)

Japan (Frazer, 84, 88, 131, 195-196, 204, 235, 585, 687, 689, 765)

Frege's Puzzle for Equality

"Equality gives rise to challenging questions…" (Frege, 3)

Frege's Puzzle (Langer)

Frankism and its Holy Mistress

"We are given to the cult of personality…" Constantine Karamanlis, Premiere of Greece

Frankism, history of (Katchen)

Connection between Frankism and the Mormon faith (Owens, part 3)

"Eva became the Frankist 'holy mistress…" (Jewish)

Fifth Mirror: Astrology and Astronomy

"It is ridiculous for us to separate…" (*Letters*, 280)

"Observation: there was absolutely nothing to see on Venus…" (Sagan)

Venus (Frazer, 402, 430)

"Yeats called it this" (Moore, 68, 169)

Venus as Lucifer (Plato)

"The word *Lucifer*" (BeliefNet)

The Maternalistic Pawnee

"All things in the world are two..." Eagle Chief (Letakos-Lesa), Pawnee. Web. http://www.firstpeople.us/FP-Html-Wisdom/EagleChief.html 4 October, 2017.

The Golden Bough (261, 501)

"The Radium Wedding of Night and Morning" (Campbell, 145)

Halley's Comet

"Aristotle's opinion... that comets were nothing else..." (Gaither, 266)

"But she did dream of comets" (*UJ*, 362) with small illustration

Sixth Mirror: The Arts and Humanities

"When archaeologists discover the missing arms of Venus de Milo..." John Barrymore

A book from Plath's library on Yeats' spiritism, *The Unicorn*, tells the story that in 1915..." (Moore, 241)

New York: Suffragette City

Mary Poppins (*UJ*, 34, 561) (*LSP*, 275, 961)

The Magic Number Seven

Netzach (Moore, 134)

(Brad Meltzer's Decoded)

"Nations, races and individual men are unified by an image..." William Butler Yeats, from "Four Years" Part XXII

"Campbell wrote that the hand" (Campbell, 192)

The Egyptian Book of the Dead

Isis's names (Frazer, 303, 421, 442-445, 492)

Compared to *Finnegans Wake* (Campbell, 72)

The German "It"

"The Awful German Language," by Mark Twain 1880

"Mark Twain's character appears frequently" (Campbell, 26)

"...suppose your statue represented her" (Fatout, 135-136)

"I came in with Halley's Comet in 1835..." by Mark Twain, 1909

Shine Little Glow-Worm, Glimmer

"Glow little glow-worm, fly of fire" lyrics by The Mills Brothers, 1952.

"Das Glühwürmchen," or "The Glow-Worm," German lyrics by Heinz Bolten-Backers. English lyrics by Lilla Cayley Robinson. Music by Paul Lincke from the operetta *Lysistrata, 1902* Web. http://perfessorbill.com/lyrics/lyglwwrm.htm 4 October 2017.

"The Disquieting Muses" (*CP*, 74)

James and the Giant Peach (Dahl)

"The great glow-worm hunt" (Independent)

"That woman, as nature has created her..." (von Sacher-Masoch)

Finnegans Wake

"10 Sephiroth of the Kabbala" (Chrisp)

"Joyce evoked the past to illuminate the present" (Joyce, 14)

"Joyce has managed, by invoking" (Joyce, 3)

"words assert a magical power over things" (Joyce, 11)

"Joyce early understood that" (Campbell, 360)

Other Feminist Forerunners

"at least two books with H.D.'s poetry" Those books are: *An Anthology of Famous English and American Poetry* (Benet, 812) and *Modern American Poetry, Modern British Poetry: a critical anthology* (Untermeyer, 16, 17, 18, 360, 387-393)

"Helen" by H.D. https://www.poetryfoundation.org/poems/46541/helen-56d22674d6e41 Web. 4 October 2017.

"Why did Virginia Woolf commit suicide?" (*UJ*, 151)

"Mrs. Dalloway" (Woolf)

"Plath wrote in 1958: 'I felt mystically...'" (*UJ*, 337)

"called him 'my boy nietzsch" (*LSP*, 780)

"my favorite philosopher" (*LSP*, 871)

Thus Spake Zarathustra (Nietzsche) The cover of this book is kept in one of Plath's scrapbooks at the Lilly Library at Indiana University-Bloomington.

Ruth Beuscher as "psychologist-priestess" (*UJ*, 338)

"...her father 'heiled Hitler' at home" (*UJ*, 430).

"I have ulcers, see how I bleed" (*UJ*, 430)

"These are my hands / My knees." (*Ariel*, 15)

"Life was hell" (*UJ*, 430)

"I do it so it feels like hell" (*Ariel*, 15)

"My mother killed the only man who'd love me steady through life" (*UJ*, 431)

"I hated men because they didn't have to suffer like a woman did" (*UJ*, 431)

References to New York, and to Jews (*UJ*, 432)

"sticky white filth of desire" (*UJ*, 432)

"Put her in a cell" (*UJ*, 432)

"stinking breath" (*UJ*, 434)

The pain of being expected to be perfect (*UJ*, 432)

Teaching Sylvia Plath's "Lady Lazarus" in the Classroom

"And now you try…" (*Ariel*, 5)

What Students Are Saying About the *Fixed Stars Govern a Life: Decoding Sylvia Plath* System:

"What I learned was that she [Sylvia Plath] fooled everyone. Her work is infinitely more complicated than people think; it's hardly about her life at all. She wrote some kind of double metaphor, building stories within stories that only the most discerning of readers would be able to determine. Plath didn't write Hemingway's metaphorical glaciers, she made Russian nesting dolls." C.A.

"I feel that I have at last met the Master Gypsy. In *Fixed Stars Govern a Life: Decoding Sylvia Plath*, by Julia Gordon-Bramer, whole new esoteric references were opened up to me. Here is a method of scholarship and a way of looking at poetry that has never before been accomplished with such depth. In poetry we read the poet and study them where they are found *in situ*, but not to this extent. Here was global learning at its best. It was not easy. There were many references that I had to research, and yet it brought my understanding to a higher level. I felt as if I had always just looked at the surface of poetry—not deep enough. As a writer of poetry it resonated with me because within my mind I could see that I pulled references when writing from the same sources as was quoted in this book. When I write consciously or subconsciously, as pointed out in *Fixed Stars Govern a Life*, I myself am drawing from my own time, my own place, historic events, my library, the things I knew, felt and studied just as Plath was." T.S.

"I became a little bit frightened, to tell you the truth. I would lie awake at night thinking about it, how connected we are and how deep everything goes. I felt like Plath in "Elm": 'I am incapable of more knowledge.' This class got in my head and I began to see the mystical patterns in everything." E.A.

"No one cares more about Sylvia Plath's works [than Gordon-Bramer]. With every assignment, there is an overview of the poem to read that week, writing tips, history and context, and of course …mysticism. It was these things that made this class easy to fall in love with. We were guided along the entire time." T.D.

"I stepped into the class on the recommendation from a friend who took the course last semester. She said that your writing, exploring Plath's writing, and the nature of the in-depth discussions would change my life. She was right. [...] This class gave me courage and the belief in my words." D.M.

"This class was designed by one of Lindenwood's best instructors, and one of the best Plath scholars anywhere, in my opinion. I feel truly honored to have learned from her. She raises the bar to a whole new level, and inspires me to be better as a writer and reader. Excellent." W.M.

"These classes are responsible for a paradigm shift in how I look at the world, and I feel that is a gift." M.D.

"Julia Gordon-Bramer does a phenomenal job of breaking down the material and providing thought provoking discussion. As someone with minimal background in poetry, I feel confident going forward as I've learned to delve deep into the multi-layers and meanings that are present." D.G.

"It is clear that these poems are not just confessional
poems. The imagery is so universal. I often found [Plath's] references in the mirrors about universal topics of war, freedom, prejudice, entrapment, infidelity, searching, truth, love and human growth and self-actualization. These topics are just as vital today as they were when she wrote them in the early sixties." T.C.

ABOUT THE AUTHOR

Julia Gordon-Bramer has been a tarot reader for nearly forty years, almost ten professionally. She received her bachelor's degree in literature and language from Webster University in St. Louis, and her MFA in creative writing (poetry and fiction) from the University of Missouri-St. Louis. While always "a Plathie," she began her serious scholarship in 2007, going farther and farther down the rabbit hole of mysticism, from which there appears to be no return. She teaches on Plath and other subjects in the Lindenwood University graduate-level creative writing program and has presented on Plath at universities and libraries across America and in the United Kingdom. In 2013, *The Riverfront Times* voted her St. Louis' Best Local Poet. In addition to the *Decoding Sylvia Plath* series (Magi Press), she is author of *Fixed Stars Govern a Life: Decoding Sylvia Plath* (2014, Stephen F. Austin State University Press) and the forthcoming *The Magician's Girl*, a biography of the mysticism of Sylvia Plath and Ted Hughes. It is Julia Gordon-Bramer's greatest wish to show the world that we haven't even scratched the surface of understanding Plath's creative genius, and more importantly, that there is something bigger going on which pulls the strings of everything.

Please give this book a review on Amazon, Goodreads, or other sites, and visit www.juliagordonbramer.com and www.magipress.co, or write DecodingSylviaPlath@gmail.com for more information.

www.ingramcontent.com/pod-product-compliance
Lightning Source LLC
Chambersburg PA
CBHW052130010526
44113CB00034B/1620